Editors

Erica N. Russikoff, M.A.

Brent L. Fox, M. Ed.

Editor in Chief

Karen J. Goldfluss, M.S. Ed.

Creative Director

Sarah M. Fournier

Cover Artists

Diem Pascarella

Barb Lorseyedi

Marilyn Goldberg

Imaging

Amanda R. Harter

Publisher

Mary D. Smith, M.S. Ed.

TCR 8088

Using and the iPad in the Classroom

- Introduces stock and third-party apps, using helpful descriptions and step-by-step directions
- Contains creative lessons and activities
- Includes extension and app-smashing ideas
- Correlated to the Common Core State Standards

Teacher Created Resources

Author

Roger Dupuy

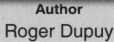

For correlations to the Common Core State Standards, see pages 93–94 of this book or visit *http://www.teachercreated.com/standards/*.

Teacher Created Resources

6421 Industry Way

Westminster, CA 92683

www.teachercreated.com

ISBN: 978-1-4206-8088-1

© 2015 Teacher Created Resources

Made in U.S.A.

TABLE OF CONTENTS

Introduction 3

First Things First 4

Wi-Fi 5

Website Permissions 5

iPad Use and Availability 5

Tags Based on Context 5

Getting Permission First 6

Switching Between, Organizing,
and Searching for Apps 7

Screen Capture 8

Select, Copy, and Paste 8

Projecting Images 9

iPad Troubleshooting 9

Let's Get to the Apps 9

Stock Apps 10

Mail 11

Timer 16

Camera 17

Dictionary 18

Safari 20

Pages 25

iMovie 31

Keynote 42

Third-Party Apps 45

Skitch 46

Let's Color! 51

Paper by FiftyThree 55

Art Lab by MoMA 59

Shadow Puppet Edu 65

Puppet Pals HD 72

Comic Life 80

Teacher Tools 84

Zite 85

Pocket 86

Sharing Services 87

iCloud 88

Dropbox 88

Box.net 90

YouTube and Vimeo 90

iPad Accessories and Care 91

Styli 92

External Bluetooth Keyboards 92

Cases 92

Stands for Teacher Use 92

Cleaning the iPad 92

Meeting Standards 93

Index 95

Using Apps and the iPad® in the Classroom is designed to help you create amazing, technology-enhanced lessons for your students. Whether you are a first-time or veteran user, this book suggests ways in which you can improve the overall classroom experience using an approachable, interactive tool.

The apps discussed in this book are divided into two categories: Stock Apps and Third-Party Apps. Stock apps are apps that Apple® provides for you. These apps come with each device or are Apple apps that can be downloaded for free from the App Store℠. They usually require Wi-Fi. Third-party apps are apps designed by other developers and can be downloaded from the App Store. These apps may require Wi-Fi and may cost a nominal fee. These recommended apps are well suited to help you deliver practical, engaging classroom lessons. In both the Stock Apps and Third-Party Apps sections, descriptions and sample lesson plans are provided.

Using Apps and the iPad® in the Classroom is your reference manual. The apps and lessons are tagged with handy descriptors to let you choose the right app for your specific curricular objectives. For example, all the app descriptions are tagged with a pedagogical context (e.g., whole class, individual, small group), grade level suggestions, and more.

In addition to extension activities, app-smashing suggestions are provided. These suggestions allow for multiple apps to be used in a single activity.

At the back of this book, you will find an index organized by these same tags. Apps are sorted by context, activity type, and alphabetically. Advice and tips for permissions, Wi-Fi, and iPad® care are also included.

Each lesson meets the digital content and collaboration components as well as other standards required by the Common Core State Standards. A list of these standards can be found on pages 93–94.

After familiarizing yourself with this book, you will find it to be an indispensable tool as you endeavor to grow in the area of technology-enhanced learning.

FIRST THINGS FIRST

Before introducing the iPad and apps in your classroom, you will want to make sure that you are properly prepared. This section contains a brief overview of basic iPad functions, including steps on how to take screenshots and suggestions for organizing and switching between apps. The importance of obtaining permission from families and school sites is also discussed. Understanding the capabilities and the parameters of your iPad before introducing it as a tool in your classroom will only make your experience as a teacher easier.

To begin, check to see how strong the Wi-Fi signal is at your school. Most schools are not ready for hundreds of simultaneous Wi-Fi logins. If your iPad app is Wi-Fi-dependent, then your experience is directly affected by how strong your school's Wi-Fi signal is. If you are at a school with little or no Wi-Fi, then you need to use your iPad differently. Look for the Wi-Fi tag under each app description. Use apps that do not require Wi-Fi. If your school has a strong Wi-Fi connection, then you will be able to use all of the apps mentioned in this book.

Wi-Fi

Schools have varying policies when it comes to website accessibility. Get a current list from your network administrator. You will need to check this list to see if the websites you plan to use are approved by your school's network administrator.

In any case, be sure to test every website on your iPad, as certain websites with Adobe® Flash® Player may not function as expected, or possibly not at all.

WEBSITE PERMISSIONS

Find out the policy on students taking the iPad home with them. Your students may not be able to do this every day. If this is the case, what apps you use will be affected. The apps in this book are tagged with useful descriptors to help you filter through what you need based on available technology.

iPAD USE AND AVAILABILITY

Teacher Research

This is your basic research and preparation. This is not at all different from what you as a teacher normally do before and after class as part of your regular preparations. The only difference is that you are including your iPad as an additional tool.

TAGS BASED ON CONTEXT

Whole Class

This is your standard whole-class, teacher-led lesson context. You will need an LCD projector and a connection cable. You will only need one iPad for this.

Small Group

This is when you are leading a small group activity (usually 2–5 people). Each student should have his or her own iPad.

Individual

This is an individual student activity. The students are all working on their own individual mobile digital devices while the teacher monitors their progress. This could also be the context for a center activity.

Note: Certain iPad activities can be used in more than one context. Also, in many cases, the activities in this book progress from whole class, to small group, to independent classwork, and finally to homework, as this would likely reflect the natural flow of the lesson.

GETTING PERMISSION FIRST

Depending on your school district's policy, you may need to get written permission from parents to take pictures of their children to display in class. It is worth the effort, as there are very creative apps that use kids' pictures. Below is an example of a letter that you can send to parents to obtain written approval for camera use in the classroom:

Dear Parent or Guardian of _____,

   Our class will be using various iPad apps during the school year. Some of the apps require the use of pictures and photos. With your permission, I would like to take photos of your child during classroom activities. These photos may be shown to other classes and administrators.

   Please sign below, indicating whether or not you agree with _____ School using digital cameras and digital images of your child for the purpose of classroom instruction.

Thank you.

_____
Teacher Signature

   ❑ I approve of you taking photos of my child.

   ❑ I do not approve of you taking photos of my child.

Parent Signature

_____

Switching between apps, especially when you're working with multiple apps, is easy to accomplish.

Organizing apps will greatly help you in the classroom. Knowing where to look for a particular app will save you valuable instructional time.

By using the Spotlight® Search function, you can search for apps quickly and efficiently.

How to Switch Between Apps (Two Ways)

1. The first way to switch between apps is to double-tap the Home button. This calls up a switching interface. It shows you the apps in the order you last used them.

2. Swipe to the left to scroll to the app you want and then tap on it to launch it.

Or

The other way is to use a four-finger swipe from right to left while having an app open (not from the Home screen). This gesture takes you to the last app you were working on. This technique is best when you are trying to jump between two or three apps.

How to Organize Apps

1. From your Home screen, tap and hold an app until all the app icons wiggle.

2. Tap and drag an app into another to create a folder, which can then be named.

3. To move an app to another screen, drag the app or folder to the edge of the screen. Be sure not to tap on the X in the upper-left corner of the app icon. This will delete the app.

4. Once you are done moving and creating folders, push the Home button. The wiggling should stop.

Suggestion: Consider designating one entire screen for teacher preparation and research; one for live, in-class demonstrations; and one for personal/private use. Creating three spaces allows you to focus on the apps that directly help you in each context.

How to Use Spotlight Search to Search for Apps

1. From the Home screen, swipe down with one finger.

2. Type what app you need.

3. Select the app.

Note: You can also use Spotlight Search for Internet searches. Simply type in what you're looking for and tap on Search Web or Search Wikipedia™.

SCREEN CAPTURE

Use your iPad to take a screenshot of the current screen display. The image is automatically saved to your Camera Roll®.

How to Use Screen Capture to Take Screenshots

1. Decide on the display of which you wish to take a photo.

2. Push the Home button and the Power button at the same time. You should hear an audible camera-clicking sound.

3. The screenshot is automatically saved to your Camera Roll.

Suggestion: Consider using Screen Capture to showcase or evaluate student work. Have students take screenshots of their progress and email them to you.

SELECT, COPY, AND PASTE

Use your iPad to select, copy, and paste text.

How to Select, Copy, and Paste Text

1. One way you can select, copy, and paste text is to tap the text you want to copy, holding your finger down until you see a magnification bubble.

2. Slide the cursor until you've highlighted all the text you intend to copy, then lift your finger.

3. Select Copy.

4. Press and hold your finger at the location where you would like to paste the text.

5. Select Paste.

The iPad can be used as a document camera. To do this, you will need a projector and either a VGA cable and Apple's VGA adapter or an HDMI cable and Apple's HDMI adapter.

If you don't want to hassle with connection cables, you can use Apple TV®. Apple TV is a small receiver that connects to your projector or TV via an HDMI cable. Using Wi-Fi, it wirelessly connects to your iPad using a feature called AirPlay®. For information on how to connect your iPad to an Apple TV, go to *http://support.apple.com/en-us/HT201335*.

Your iPad is very reliable; however, there are two common problems that your iPad may have. The first one can be referred to as the "Sudden Quit." This occurs when you are working in one of your apps and, suddenly, the app quits. If this happens, you will need to restart the app. During a "Sudden Quit," you may lose some of the data. (e.g., Some of your Pages® document might not have been saved.)

The second problem can be referred to as the "Freeze." This is when an app stops working, and no amount of tapping can unfreeze it. If this happens, try pushing the Home button first. If this doesn't work, push the Power button (at the top-right corner of your iPad). If neither of these work, then you will need to restart your device.

How to Restart Your Device

1. Hold the Power button until "slide to power off" appears. Follow these instructions. Once the device is off, press the Power button to turn it back on.

2. If you can't restart your device, reset it by pressing and holding the Power and Home buttons at the same time until the Apple logo appears.

Note: When all else fails, go to *support.apple.com* for the latest information on solving your issue.

Suffice it to say, the iPad has the foundational functionality to be a very useful tool. The rest of this book is designed to show how it can benefit you while suggesting apps, lessons, and activities that you can use in your classroom.

PROJECTING IMAGES

IPAD TROUBLESHOOTING

LET'S GET TO THE APPS

Stock Apps

This section introduces features of stock apps for the iPad. Stock apps are apps that Apple provides for you. These apps come with each device or are Apple apps that can be downloaded for free from the App Store. They may require Wi-Fi. Learning how to use these stock apps will prepare you to most effectively implement the other apps introduced in this book.

MAIL

Description

Mail® is Apple's email program. The Mail app is essential to the functionality of the iPad because it is the main sharing mechanism. Upon receiving your iPad, set up one or more email accounts for classroom use.

How to Set Up a Mail (Email) Account

1. Launch the Settings app.

2. On the left side of the screen, select Mail, Contacts, Calendars.

3. Under the Accounts heading, select Add Account. Several email options will appear. The steps are slightly different depending on the account you wish to use. The next page explains how to set up a Gmail™ account.

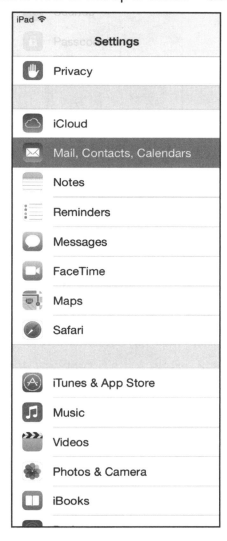

TAGS

Free

Classroom Contexts: Whole Class, Teacher Research, Individual, Small Group

Wi-Fi: required to receive and send emails; Wi-Fi not needed to read, organize, and compose messages

Grades: all

Prerequisites: none

Developer: Apple Inc.

MAIL

How to Set Up a Mail (Email) Account *(cont.)*

    a. Select Google™ for a Gmail account.

    b. Enter your name, full email address, email password, and a short description.

    c. Select Next.

    d. Decide which services you would like tied to your Gmail account. Toggle the button sliders once you've made your choices.

How to Send a Mail Email

1. Launch the Mail app.

2. Select the "compose" icon (it looks like a box with a pen pointing to the middle of it) to open a new Mail composing window.

3. Tap on the To section. Enter the email address of the recipient.

4. Tap on the Subject section. Enter your subject.

5. Type a short message. Remind your students to always include their names.

6. Review your email.

7. Tap the Send button in the upper-right corner of the composition window.

MAIL

Some Mail Tips

From within the Mail composing window, if you tap on From, you will be able to choose from all the email accounts (personal, work, etc.) you have set up on your iPad.

From the main Mail view screen, if you tap and hold (also known as a "long press") the Compose icon, all of your unsent drafts will appear.

Wi-Fi and Email

You can compose emails without a Wi-Fi connection. Once you are in a Wi-Fi hotspot, your emails will be sent automatically.

The Subject Line

Stress the importance of a strong subject line with your students. You will be getting plenty of emails, and you need to quickly determine from the subject line what the emails are about. Many of the apps in this book will require that your students send you attachments. It's important that they include subject lines to alert you to specific assignments.

Your Choice: One or Many Email Accounts

Decide whether you are going to have each of your students set up a separate email account or if you will only have a single email account for the whole class. Separate email accounts make more sense for older students. You still may need to set up each of their email accounts for them. This will likely take some time, but it's essential. Your students may not be too familiar with the iPad, and knowing how to send emails is one of the first things you need to teach them. Remember that many of the apps in this book require email to share and submit files. If you decide to use a single email account for the whole class, then you will still need to set up this email account on each iPad.

 MAIL

Send an Email Introduction to Your Teacher

Lesson Objective

Students will learn how to send emails introducing themselves. Students will learn basic email etiquette.

Materials and Preparation

- one iPad per student
- one teacher iPad and projection or streaming technology

Prepare an introduction of yourself on a piece of notebook paper. Here is a sample self-introduction for your students:

> Dear Ms./Mr. _____,
>
> My name is _____. I am _____ years old. I have _____ members in my family. My favorite food is _____ _____, and my favorite color is _____.
> My favorite hobby is _____.
> I'm happy to be in your class.
>
> Sincerely,
>
> _____

Opening/Input

1. Tell your students that you are happy to be their teacher and that in order to have a great year, it would be a good idea to get to know each other. Then tell them that you are going to start by sending an email to introduce yourself to them.

2. Send an email using the steps listed in "How to Send a Mail Email" (page 12).

Guided Practice

Ask a volunteer to go through the same steps that you just went through to send an email. Monitor to ensure the student is including every step.

On Their Own

Have students send introductory emails to you.

App-Smashing

Have each student draw a picture using the app Paper by FiftyThree or Art Lab and then send you the file using Mail.

MAIL

Sending and Receiving Attachments

This is one of the primary ways to get data in and out of the iPad. The files going in and out are called attachments. The following instructions explain how to send files that you want to share.

How to Send Image Files

1. Launch the Photos® app. In the upper-left corner, you can view your photos by Moments, Collections, and Years.

2. Select a photo from Moments.

3. Tap on the "share" icon (it looks like a box with an arrow pointing out of the top of it). A tray of icons representing all your sharing options will appear.

4. Select the "Mail" icon and proceed with sending your email.

How to Send Notes

1. Launch the Notes® app. Create a document.

2. Select the "share" icon in the upper-right corner of the screen.

3. Select the "Mail" icon and proceed with sending your email.

How to Send Files from Pages, Keynote®, and Numbers®

1. Launch the Pages (Apple's word-processing app), Keynote (Apple's presentation app), or Numbers (Apple's spreadsheet app) app. Create a document.

2. Select the "share" icon in the upper-right corner. Choose Send a Copy. A tray of icons representing your sharing options will appear.

3. Select the desired format. Pages will give you format choices such as Pages, PDF, Word®, or ePub. Keynote will give you format choices such as Keynote, PDF, or PowerPoint®. Numbers will give you format choices such as Numbers, PDF, Excel®, or CSV.

4. Select the "Mail" icon and proceed with sending your email.

How to Open Files Received Via Email

1. Launch the Mail app, and select an email that has an attachment.

2. Press and hold the "attachment" icon. A pop-up menu will display a list of apps capable of opening the attachment (i.e., Mail, Pages, Google Drive™).

3. Select the app you want to use to open the file.

TIMER

Description

Your iPad has a stock Clock® app with a built-in timer. Use it to time the activities in your lessons. There is a quick way to get the timer to launch.

How to Launch the Clock App

1. On the iPad screen, swipe up to see the Settings tray.

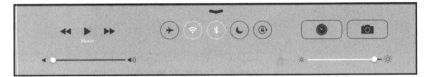

2. Select the "clock" icon on the right side of the tray.
3. Within the big circle, swipe up or down to set the minutes and/or hours.
4. Press the Start button on the left.

Or

1. Select the Clock app.
2. Select Timer in the bottom-right part of the screen.
3. Continue with steps 3–4 above.

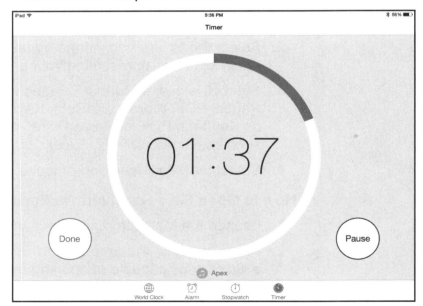

Note: You can choose different alarm tones by selecting the center "music note" icon.

CAMERA

Description

The Camera® app is one of the most important apps included on the iPad because of its universality. You can use the Camera app to take regular-sized or square pictures (including self-portraits) and regular or time-lapse videos. The Camera app can also be used as a document camera.

How to Take Pictures and Videos

1. Power on your iPad, using either the Power button on the upper-right corner or the Home button on the bottom front of your iPad.

2. Swipe up the small "camera" icon located in the bottom-right corner of the screen.

3. Select whether you want to take a time-lapse video, regular video, regular photo, or square photo.

4. Compose your shot. For photos, zoom in using the slider bar at the bottom of the screen, or by placing two fingers onto the screen and spreading them apart.

5. Tap the large dot on the right of the screen (white for photo, red for video).

6. The photo or video is now saved to your Camera Roll. You can access this photo or video from the Photos app.

Or

1. Launch the Camera app.

2. Continue with steps 3–6 above.

Other Useful Camera Features

- To take a self-portrait, tap the "camera switch" icon in the upper-right corner of the screen. This will switch from the back camera to the front camera.

- To adjust the lighting, tap on the subject or area of focus.

- To take successive snapshots automatically, tap and hold down the large white dot while taking a picture.

- To take a delayed picture, tap on the "timer" icon on the right of the screen.

TAGS

Free

Classroom Contexts: Whole Class, Teacher Research, Individual, Small Group

Wi-Fi: not required

Grades: all

Prerequisites: none

Developer: Apple Inc.

DICTIONARY

Description

Although not an app, this feature allows you to highlight any text on the iPad and look it up using Dictionary®.

How to Search for the Definition of a Word

1. Highlight a word by either double-tapping it or pressing and holding it.

2. Select Define from the pop-up options.

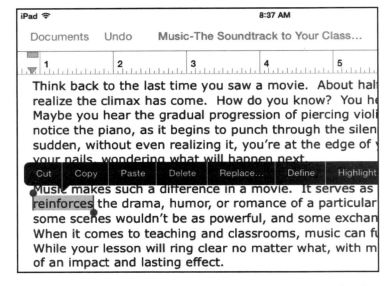

3. A pop-up window with a detailed dictionary definition will appear. Scroll down for more details on the entry, including etymology.

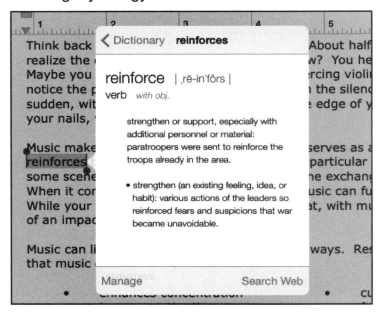

Double-Tap Dictionary Word Search

Lesson Objective

Students will learn how to use the stock dictionary feature to get definitions of teacher-selected vocabulary words.

Materials and Preparation

- one iPad per student
- one teacher iPad and projection or streaming technology

Using Pages, prepare a list of ten vocabulary words of which your students need to learn the definitions. Display the list from your iPad onto a screen using a projector.

Opening/Input

1. Open the Pages document that lists your ten vocabulary words. Use the projector to display the Pages word list.

2. For each vocabulary word, show how to double-tap the word to get the pop-up menu with the Define feature. Select Define.

3. Read the definition, and then tap on the Pages document next to the vocabulary word and record the definition from memory. You may have to double-tap on the vocabulary word more than once to verify the definition.

Guided Practice

Have a student repeat the Opening/Input with your guidance.

On Their Own

1. Instruct students to complete steps 1–3 from the Opening/Input on their own.

2. Once they are done, they should email their Pages documents to you.

Extensions

- Show your students how to use the stock dictionary feature in other cases. For instance, any website text can be highlighted and looked up using this feature. Press and hold the word to pop up the Define option.

- By selecting Manage on the definition page, you can download other dictionary databases, including language translation dictionaries. You can also search online resources such as Google to find a definition.

SAFARI

Description

Safari® is Apple's Web browser. Use it to search the Web for information.

How to Use Safari

1. Launch the Safari app.

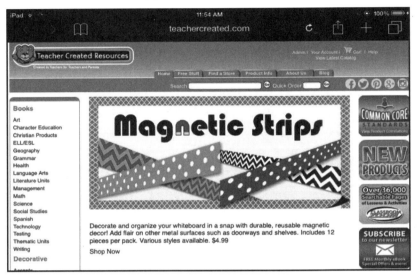

2. Tap on the URL window and type in a Web address or search term.

Safari Features

In the upper-left corner, you will find the backward and forward arrows, as well as the "Bookmarks" icon. The Bookmarks feature allows you to save websites to your Favorites or Reading Lists. It also stores any Shared Links, which are links shared by your contacts from specific social networks.

SAFARI

Safari Features *(cont.)*

Inside the URL window is the "reload" icon, followed by the "share" icon. If you tap on the "share" icon (it has an arrow pointing up inside a box), a tray of icons representing all your sharing options will appear. Tap on this icon to bookmark or add a site to your Reading List.

Select the "plus" icon to view an additional website. To view all of your websites at once, select the icon with overlapping squares.

Saving Images and Text

While you are browsing, you can tap on and hold almost any image to save it to the Camera Roll. You can also highlight and copy text to paste into other apps.

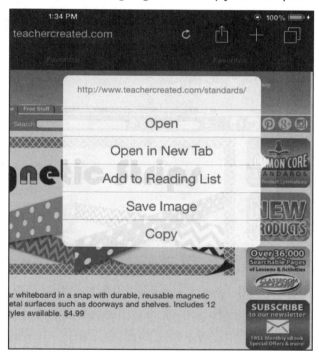

Creating Shortcut Icons

You can create a shortcut icon for any website you frequent. This is particularly useful when you are preparing a lesson and would like to have all of your websites in one place. You can create a folder on the Home screen with all the shortcut icons you need. Having a shortcut icon saves time. Instead of launching Safari and selecting a bookmark, you can just tap on the desired shortcut icon on your Home screen.

How to Create a Shortcut Icon

1. When you are viewing the website for which you want to have a shortcut, tap on the "share" icon.

2. Select the Add to Home button.

3. A pop-up window will appear, allowing you to edit the title of your new shortcut icon. Once you've decided on a title, select Add.

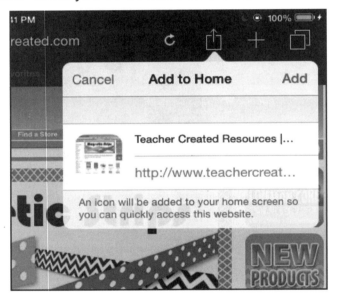

Protecting Your Students from Websites with a Lot of Clutter

Some websites are very cluttered with extraneous text, ads, and other distractions. You can instantly clean up the viewing interface by selecting the Reader button (it looks like a set of horizontal lines) that is inside and to the left of the URL text window.

Note: Not all websites work with this.

SAFARI

Gathering Information/Research

Lesson Objective

Students will create Pages documents, search the Internet for pictures, and then add the pictures to the Pages documents.

Materials and Preparation

- one iPad per student
- one teacher iPad and projection or streaming technology

Prepare a shortcut icon of the website *http://animalphotos.info* or any other photo-rich website of animals.

Opening/Input

1. Tell students, "When you get older, you will need to be 'information treasure hunters.' Let's practice being one now."

2. Show students images of animals by browsing through the animal website chosen in Preparation.

3. Choose an animal and save the image to your Photo Library. Make sure you audibly share your thinking process.

4. Create a Pages document.

5. Type the name of the animal onto the document.

6. Add the image of the animal to the document by tapping on the "plus" icon and selecting the "landscape" icon (it looks like a mountain and the sun inside of a rectangle). Select Recently Added. Then select the picture.

7. Tap on Blank to rename the document "[your name]'s [animal]."

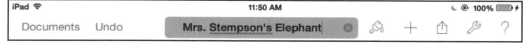

8. Have students think-pair-share what their favorite animals are.

SAFARI

Guided Practice

Choose a student volunteer to go through steps 3–7 with his/her animal of choice. Use the four-finger app-switching technique to quickly switch from the website to the Pages document and back again.

On Their Own

1. Zoom in on the URL so it is big enough for all your students to see.

2. Project steps 3–7 onto a screen for your students to refer to and stay on task.

3. Set the iPad timer for an appropriate amount of time for your students to find and save their animals' images to their Photo Libraries. Switch back to the list of steps. Then walk around and monitor progress.

4. Invite a few students to share their favorite animals with the rest of the class.

Extension and App-Smashing

- Challenge your students by having them write more than the animal's name in the documents. They can write one or more sentences describing their animals.

- Send your students the URL via email first, and have them go to the URL from within the Mail app. Or have students email their documents to you or other classmates. This makes the activity more complex because they are having to use the Mail app.

PAGES

Description

Pages is Apple's word processor. Its simple interface makes it ideal for young pre-writers and writers. Learning how to use Pages is important, as it is the foundation for many of the other lessons and activities in this book.

How to Use Pages as a Word Processor

1. Launch the Pages app.
2. Select Create Document.

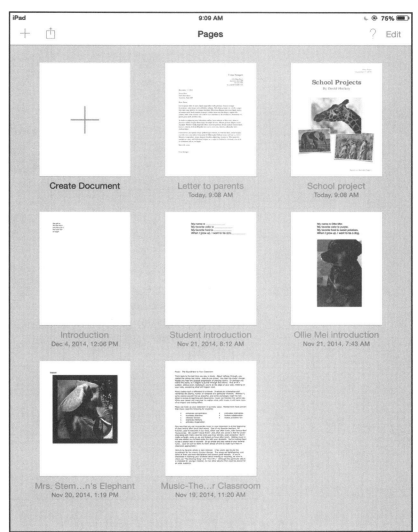

How to Use Pages as a Word Processor *(cont.)*

3. Choose a template.

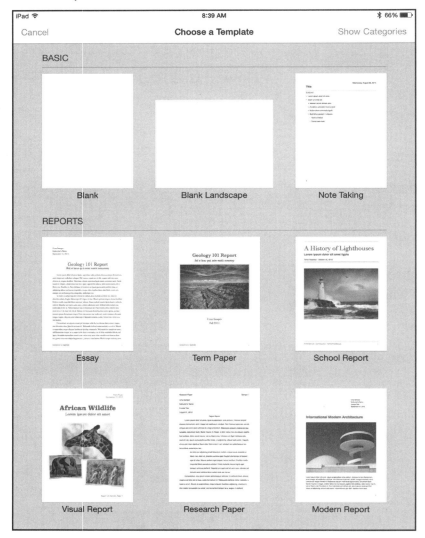

4. Rename the file by tapping on Blank and adding your own file name.

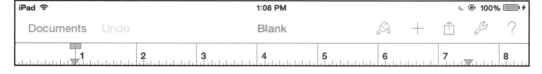

Other Useful Pages Features

- For simple formatting, select the options at the bottom of the screen. Alternatively, you can select the "paintbrush" icon in the upper-right corner of the screen.

- Pages automatically saves. To view or revise an existing document, you must first access the file system.

PAGES

How to Access the File System in Pages

1. Launch the Pages app or select Documents in the upper-left corner of the screen from within the Pages app. All of your documents will appear as thumbnails.

2. Tap on the file you want to open.

Note: To rename a file, tap on the file name.

How to Create Document Folders in Pages

1. Launch the Pages app or select Documents in the upper-left corner of the screen from within the Pages app. All of your documents will appear as thumbnails.

2. Tap and hold one of the documents and hover it over another document. A folder will appear.

3. Release your finger to drop the document into the folder.

4. Rename the folder by typing in the white text box.

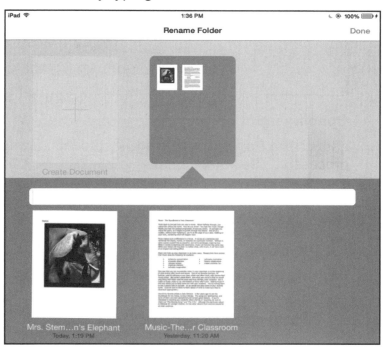

5. Tap outside the folder to close it.

How to Add an Image to a Pages Document

1. Select the "plus" icon in the upper-right corner of the screen.

2. Select one of the Albums.

3. Choose an image.

4. Drag and resize the image as needed.

PAGES

Writing a Self-Introduction

Lesson Objective

Students will learn how to create a Pages document using basic formatting.

Materials and Preparation

- one iPad per student
- one teacher iPad and projection or streaming technology

Prepare an introduction template (first on paper and then on the iPad) for students to follow. Here's an example for you to use:

iPad 🛜	8:07 AM	🔋 100% ⚡
Documents Undo	Blank	

My name is _____.
My favorite color is _____.
My favorite food is _____.
When I grow up, I want to be a(n)_____.

Opening/Input

Launch the Pages app and show students how to use Pages as a word processor. (See steps on pages 25–26.) Model each step.

Guided Practice

Have a student volunteer perform the steps you just demonstrated.

On Their Own

1. Display the steps for how to use Pages as a word processor.
2. Have students launch the Pages app and introduce themselves using the introduction template.

Extensions

- Show students how to format or edit text, and then allow them to practice.
- Have your students email their introductions to you.
- Have students email their introductions to classmates.

PAGES

Writing a Self-Introduction with Images

Lesson Objective

Students will learn how to create a Pages document using basic formatting skills and an image. This is an extension of the Self-Introduction lesson.

Materials and Preparation

- one iPad per student
- one teacher iPad and projection or streaming technology

The example below uses the template that was created in the previous lesson. For this lesson, you are going to add an image as shown.

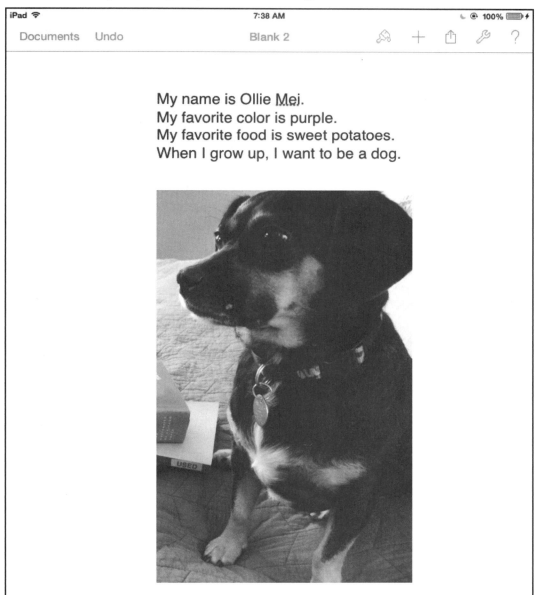

PAGES

Opening/Input

1. Launch the Pages app and show students how to use Pages as a word processor. (See steps on pages 25–26.) Model each step.

2. Tell students that they will be adding pictures of themselves to their documents.

3. Demonstrate how to take a picture using the Camera app.

4. Show how to add an image to a Pages document. (See page 27.)

Guided Practice

Have a student volunteer perform the steps you just demonstrated.

On Their Own

1. Tell students to take pictures of themselves using the Camera app.

2. Instruct students to launch the Pages app and introduce themselves using the introduction template.

3. Have them follow the steps to add images to Pages documents.

Extensions and App-Smashing

- Have your students email their introductions to you or their classmates.

- Have students choose a different Pages template. For example, they can create classroom posters using one of the Flyers & Posters templates or create invitations using one of the Cards templates.

iMovie

Description

iMovie® is Apple's video-editing and movie-making app. Although this app is most likely too difficult to be taught to K–2 students, teachers can still use it as a teaching tool in the classroom.

Any photo or movie shared to the Photo Library or taken by your iPad can be used in iMovie. Also, iMovie has preloaded stock music, sound effects, and visual effects available for use in your movie creation. You can also download other music via your iTunes® account.

The app's interface reveals just enough detail for the basic functionality. If you want to utilize other, more advanced features, they can be easily accessed and are not too difficult to navigate. The information and steps provided here are designed to introduce the basic features of the app in small, manageable pieces.

There are two basic ways to use iMovie—as an iMovie Project and as a Trailer.

TAGS

Free

Classroom Contexts: Whole Class, Teacher Research

Wi-Fi: optional (for uploading movies)

Grade: n/a

Prerequisites: familiarity with the Camera app

Developer: Apple Inc.

App Version: 2.1.1

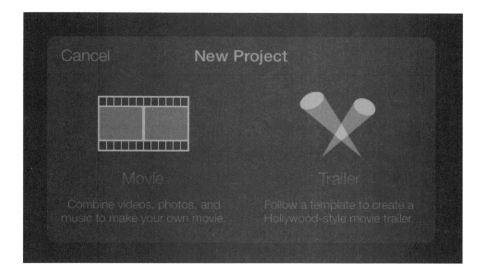

iMOVIE

How to Create a Movie

1. Launch the iMovie app.

2. Tap on the "plus" icon in the upper-right corner of the screen.

3. Select Movie.

4. Select one of the templates displayed at the bottom of the screen. iMovie gives you an array of templates to choose from. To see a preview of each, highlight the desired template and tap the "play" icon. Beginners may want to start with the Simple template.

5. In the upper-right corner of the screen, select Create. This is the basic movie editing screen.

6. Tap on Photos to search through the images in your Photo Library. After finding a photo to include in your movie, tap on the image to move it to your project timeline at the bottom of the screen.

7. Similarly, tap on Video to choose from prerecorded movie clips. Tap the "play" icon to preview the video, or tap the downward arrow to add it to your timeline.

iMovie

How to Create a Movie *(cont.)*

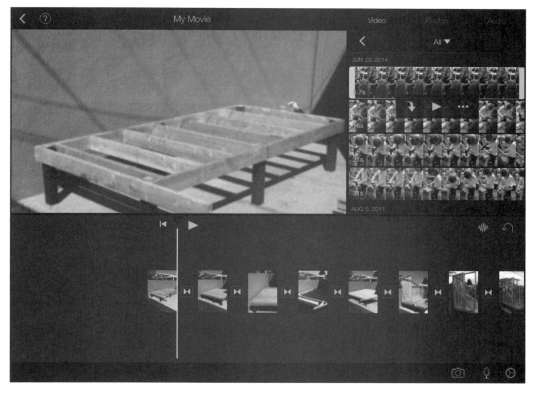

8. Locate where the "undo" icon is. It looks like a U-turn arrow. It is located on the right side of the screen, just above the project timeline. Use it whenever you want to undo the last thing you did.

9. At any point you want to remove a photo or video clip, you can also use the Delete feature. First, tap on the photo or video in the bottom timeline that you would like to remove. When the item is highlighted, tap on the "scissors" icon in the bottom-left corner of the screen. Three options will appear in the bottom-right of the screen: Split, Duplicate, and Delete. Tap on Delete to make the selected item disappear.

10. You can change the order of your video clips and photos by holding down your finger on the image and dragging it to a different place on the timeline. (You can do this with audio clips as well).

11. Preview your movie by pressing the "play" icon at the beginning of the timeline.

Note: Your movie is still in the project mode. This means that your movie can still be edited. You can share this current version at any time; however, once this current version is shared, the shared version cannot be edited anymore. Remember that you still have your original "project" available to edit and share as a different, perhaps more complete, version later.

Sharing Your iMovie

Tap on the "arrow" icon in the upper-left part of the screen. Next, tap on the My Movie text to rename your movie project. From here you can choose from several icons: "play," "share," "delete," or you can return to the "editing" mode.

To share this project, select the "share" icon (it looks like an arrow pointing up inside a box). You will have the option to share your movie project to iMovie Theater®, Facebook, YouTube™, Vimeo, Messages®, or Mail, as well as your own Photo Library or iTunes account.

Various Sharing Options

Sharing to YouTube

This works great with finished movie projects that are too large to send via email. In order to save to YouTube, you will need to first set up a free YouTube video channel account. Once this is done, you can send URLs to others wanting to view your videos. If you prefer to keep your videos private, you can make them accessible only to the recipient of the URL generated by YouTube.

 iMOVIE

Various Sharing Options *(cont.)*

Sharing to Vimeo

Similar to YouTube, Vimeo allows the user to post private videos and send customized URLs to others. Vimeo caters to a generally higher quality set of hosted videos.

Sharing to Facebook

Users must have a Facebook account before posting or sharing videos on this site. Facebook is not recommended for school policy reasons (school blacklists, etc.), and it's very hard to make the hosted videos private. Sharing to Facebook is not recommended for these reasons.

Sharing to iMovie Theater

This is a great option if you have a school iCloud® account. The videos shared to iMovie Theater are available to anyone who shares the same iCloud account. Using iMovie Theater with your personal iCloud account is not recommended. You will soon run out of hosting space.

Sharing to iTunes

Sharing to iTunes has the same issues as iMovie Theater. You don't want to get in the habit of using your personal accounts for potentially large iMovie files.

Sharing as a Message

For school purposes, this option is not advised.

Going Deeper

You can edit your project by adding more photos and video clips, changing the length of these clips, and adding audio files and sound effects. You can also add text to your movie, adjust transitions, slow down or speed up a clip, zoom in and crop your video clips and photos, and more. Let's explore some of these fun features.

Trimming Video Clips

If you want to trim the length of a video clip to edit out extraneous footage, first highlight the clip by tapping on the image in the timeline at the bottom of the screen. You should see a yellow box around the image. Next, place your finger on the left, heavy, yellow-colored bar and drag it to the right to exclude footage at the beginning of the clip; drag your finger on the right, heavy, yellow-colored bar to the left to exclude footage at the end of the clip. If you need to trim out footage in the middle of a clip, use the white line as a guide and drag the clip close to where you want to trim out footage. Make sure the clip is highlighted, and then select the Split button at the bottom of the screen. This splits the original clip into two clips. Then, just as above, use the yellow bars on the right and left of the clip to cut out undesired footage.

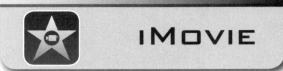

iMOVIE

Adding Text to Your Movie

Tap on a movie clip or photo in your timeline. Next, tap on the "text" (T) icon in the bottom-left corner of the screen. Several formatting options will appear on the bottom of the screen. Choose the format you wish to use by tapping on the appropriate box. "Title Text Here" will appear over your image, prompting you to replace the words with your own personalized text. Tap the "play" icon to preview your added text.

Adding Audio to Your Movie

More than likely, your video clips already contain sound from the original recordings. If you want to keep the original audio, you don't need to do anything. However, if you'd like to add to or replace the existing audio, you can easily add a voice-over audio clip. Here's how it is done.

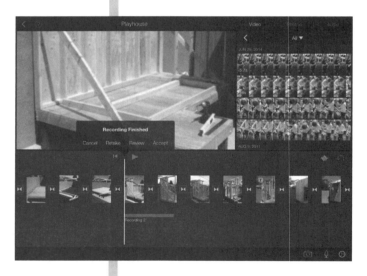

How to Add a Voice-Over Audio Clip

1. Swipe your finger to any location on your timeline. Tap the "microphone" icon in the bottom-right corner of the app, and a recording prompt will appear.

2. Tap Record, and a countdown to record your voice will begin. Start speaking after the word Recording appears.

3. When you are done, select Stop. This gives you four options: Accept, Review, Retake, and Cancel.

4. Select Accept to add your voice-over to your timeline.

5. Select Review to hear how your voice-over will sync with the rest of the timeline.

6. Select Retake to start the recording process over again. The previous voice-over will be deleted.

7. Select Cancel to remove the voice-over prompt and return to the iMovie editing screen.

iMOVIE

How to Adjust the Volume Level of the Audio Clip

1. Tap on a clip in the timeline.

2. Select Audio in the bottom-left corner of the screen. You can raise or lower the audio volume of the clip. Just slide the volume level left or right to decrease or increase the volume.

How to Use the Fade Feature

The Fade feature gives you the ability to gradually increase or decrease the volume at the beginning or end of a clip. If your iMovie video clip finishes before the music, you will likely want to fade out the music (or else the sudden end of your movie can be a bit jarring). Just slide the downward-facing triangles to taper the volume.

Trimming Your Audio Clips

The audio clip can be trimmed in the same way as a video clip.

How to Detach the Audio from the Video Clip

1. Tap on a video clip in the timeline.

2. Select the "scissors" icon in the bottom-left corner of the screen, then tap Detach in the bottom-right corner of the screen. The audio and the video files are now two separate files. You can now adjust the volume and speed up or slow down the clip to create funny effects. (However, the main reason for detaching audio from a video clip is to pair the audio with a different video clip or photo on your timeline and have it act, in effect, as a voice-over.)

Adding Other Audio Types: Music and Sound Effects

Select Audio in the upper-right corner of the app. All of your sound and music options will appear below.

 iMOVIE

How to Add Background Music from the Stock Templates

1. Tap on Theme Music and select a theme. You can preview it by tapping on the "play" icon.

2. If you like it, you can tap on the downward arrow icon. A green-colored audio clip image will now appear on your timeline. (You can now edit this audio clip in the same way you can edit other audio clips.)

Adding Sound Effects to Your Timeline

There are more than 60 stock sound effects included in iMovie. To add a sound effect, swipe your finger to move your timeline to the exact spot where you want to add a sound. Next, choose a sound effect and either press the "play" icon to preview it, or tap the downward arrow icon to add it to your timeline.

Adding Music to Your Timeline

You can also add sound recordings created with other apps, as well as imported or downloaded music (organized by playlist, album, artist, or song from your iTunes library).

iMovie Project Ideas for Teachers

Student and Classroom Portfolios

Any screenshot you take on your iPad can be added to your iMovie project timeline. Take screenshots of your students' completed work over time, and you can drop these photos into your timeline to create a student portfolio montage. Similarly, you can create a classroom portfolio montage by dropping in photographs of all the different assignments and projects completed throughout the year. Play the iMovie at year end to celebrate the students' progress.

Instructional Videos

Create a step-by-step instructional video of a long-term project by showing each step and recording a voice-over explaining the various stages of the project. Post the video online as a way for students and parents to preview a project, or as an instructional guide to be used while completing a project.

iMOVIE

How to Create a Trailer Using iMovie

1. Launch the iMovie app.

2. Tap on the "plus" icon in the upper-right corner of the screen.

3. Select Trailer.

4. Select one of the templates displayed at the bottom of the screen. iMovie gives you an array of movie themes to choose from (Superhero, Adrenaline, Family, etc.). To see a preview of each, highlight the desired template and tap the "play" icon. The length of the movie trailer and the suggested number of "actors" are displayed under the selected trailer.

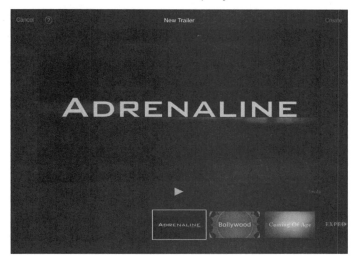

5. In the upper-right corner of the screen, select Create. This will take you to the trailer Outline and Storyboard.

6. Tap on each line in the Outline to customize the credits screen, including the name of the movie, the name of the studio, and the names of the people involved.

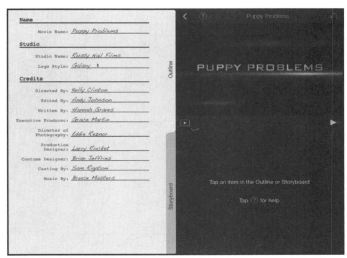

iMOVIE

How to Create a Trailer Using iMovie *(cont.)*

7. After you have completed your credits page, tap on the Storyboard tab. Here you will see a scene-by-scene breakdown of the entire trailer. To add text, tap on the blue highlighted lines and replace the existing text. You can use the original text as a guide to help you develop your own story.

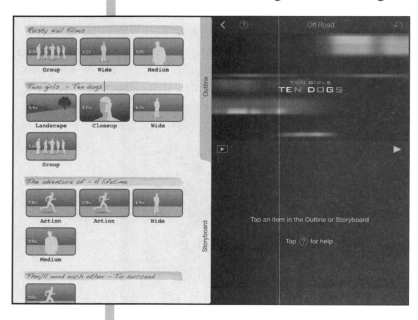

8. Next, tap on one of the gray photo boxes on the left to highlight it in blue. On the right half of your screen, you will be given several options from where you can choose what photos or videos you would like to use. In the bottom-right corner, you will see three choices: Video, Photos, and Camera. Tap on Video if you would like to add a video clip, or tap on Photos if you would prefer to add a still image.

9. To use an existing photo or video, tap on the image, and it will be added to the highlighted box.

If you would like to use a new video or photo, choose Camera and then proceed to use the Camera as you normally would. After you take a new video or photo, the scene will automatically be added to your trailer. To delete the video or photo, tap on the new image and then the "trash" icon.

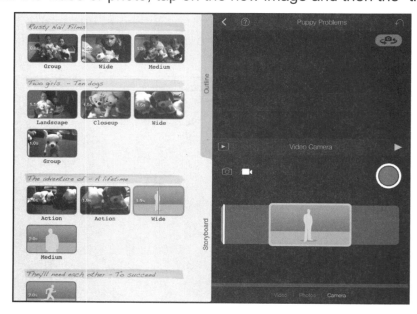

iMOVIE

How to Create a Trailer Using iMovie *(cont.)*

10. To edit a photo or video once it has been placed onto the storyboard, tap the image on the storyboard to bring up the editing screen on the right side of the page. Follow the directions on the screen to fine-tune photos and videos. Swipe with one finger to move the position of the photo, and pinch with two fingers to zoom in and out. For videos, swipe with one finger to adjust which portion of the clip is used.

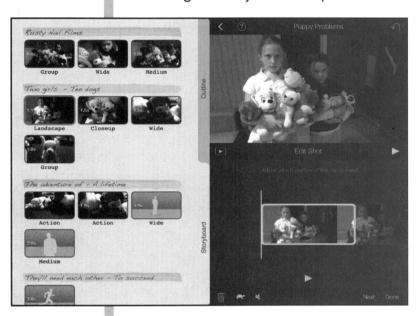

11. Add and delete text, photos, and videos until you have filled every space on the storyboard. You can tap the "play" icon at any point during the construction of your trailer to view its current status.

12. When you have finished, tap on the "arrow" icon in the top center of the screen. Your trailer is now complete (although it can still be edited). From here, you can choose from several icons: "play," "share," "delete," or you can return to the "editing" mode. To share this project, select the "share" icon. You will have the option of sharing your movie project to iMovie Theater, Facebook, YouTube, Vimeo, Messages, or Mail, as well as your own Photo Library or iTunes account.

Description

Keynote is Apple's presentation app. Although this app is too difficult to be taught to K–2 students, teachers can still use it as a teaching tool in the classroom. Keynote presentations can be exported as PDFs, Keynote files, or Microsoft® PowerPoint files. In addition, Microsoft PowerPoint files can be opened as Keynote files.

How to Create a Keynote Presentation

1. Launch the Keynote app.

2. Tap the "plus" icon in the upper-left corner and select Create Presentation.

3. Choose from one of the themes displayed. Keynote gives you an array of themes from which to choose. Beginners should choose one of the first three themes in the top row.

4. The first slide shown is a title slide. Double-tap inside the first text box and title your presentation.

TAGS

Free

Classroom Contexts: Whole Class, Teacher Research

Wi-Fi: optional (for sharing files)

Grade: n/a

Prerequisites: familiarity with Mail, Camera, and Safari apps

Developer: Apple Inc.

App Version: 2.5.2

KEYNOTE

How to Create a Keynote Presentation *(cont.)*

5. To add a new slide, tap on the boxed "plus" icon in the bottom-left corner of the screen. This produces a selection tray of different slide layouts. Choose the layout that suits you.

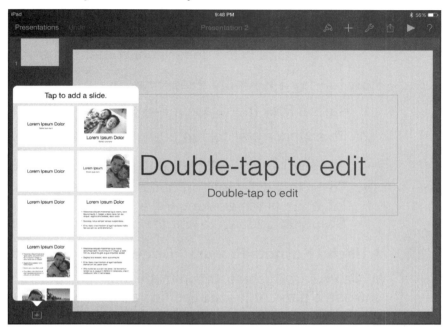

6. Tap on the "plus" icon in the upper-right corner of the screen to see a set of options, which includes adding images, shapes, or text. Use pinch and zoom to resize shapes. To resize images, tap on the image to reveal small blue guide dots. Drag these dots to resize the image.

How to Create a Keynote Presentation *(cont.)*

7. When you are finished adding text and images, tap on Presentations in the upper-left corner of the screen. This will take you back to the file view screen.

8. Tap on the default name beneath the thumbnail image of your newly created Keynote presentation. Enter the name for the file. Once you are finished, tap on Done in the upper-right corner of the screen.

How to Play a Keynote Presentation

1. Tap on Play (right-facing triangle) in the upper-right corner of the screen.

2. To advance a slide, tap or swipe on the left side.

3. To return to the previous slide, swipe to the right.

4. To go to a different part of the presentation, swipe your finger from the left edge of the screen, and a mini display of all your slides will appear. Swipe up or down to find the particular slide you are looking for.

A Useful Keynote Feature: Drawing and Using the Laser Pointer

While you are in presentation mode, tap and hold your finger on the screen until you see a pane of "pencil tips" in various colors. These allow you to draw on your slides during a presentation. On the far left is the "laser pointer" option. When you select this, a laser dot will appear on the audience's projected screen. Use this option to draw attention to a specific area on a slide.

How to Email a Keynote Presentation

1. Tap on the "share" icon.

2. Select Send a Copy.

3. Choose your desired format—Keynote, PDF, or PowerPoint.

4. Select Mail.

5. A new message will appear. Enter a recipient, subject line, and message.

THIRD-PARTY APPS

THIS SECTION INTRODUCES FEATURES OF THIRD-PARTY APPS. THIRD-PARTY APPS ARE APPS DESIGNED BY DEVELOPERS OTHER THAN APPLE AND CAN BE DOWNLOADED FROM THE APP STORE. THESE APPS MAY REQUIRE WI-FI AND MAY COST A NOMINAL FEE. THESE RECOMMENDED APPS ARE WELL SUITED TO HELP YOU DELIVER PRACTICAL, ENGAGING CLASSROOM LESSONS.

SKITCH

Description

Skitch is an efficient image-annotation tool. It can be used during a lesson to mark-up an image while teaching. It can also be used by your students to annotate images from the Web or photos they took using their devices. The annotated images can be shared, saved to the Photo Library, or opened up in another app.

How to Annotate an Image

1. Launch the Skitch app.

2. Skitch will call up your Photo Library. From here, you can select an image you want to annotate. Alternatively, you can swipe to Camera at the bottom of the screen to launch the Camera app. From here, you can snap a picture to use.

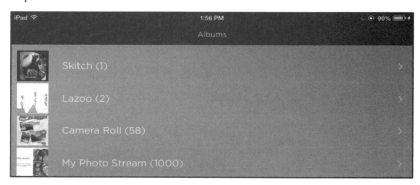

3. Tap the part of the image where you want the arrow to begin. Then, without lifting up your finger, swipe in the direction you want the arrow to point. Should you make a mistake, just tap on the "undo" icon at the top of the screen.

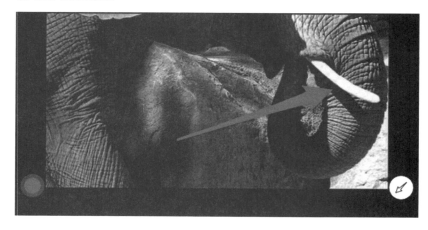

 SKITCH

How to Annotate an Image *(cont.)*

4. To add text to describe what your newly created arrow is pointing at, tap the arrow button on the right side of the app. A menu will appear.

5. Select the text tool—it looks like a lowercase letter *a*.

6. Tap on the point in your image where you want your text to appear.

7. Type your text. When finished, tap outside of the text box.

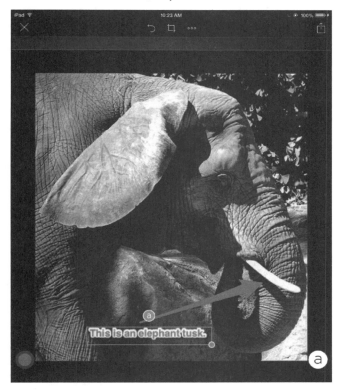

8. You are now ready to share or save your newly annotated image. To do this, tap on the "share" icon. A tray of sharing options will appear. To save the image, swipe to Save at the bottom of the screen. Several save options will appear.

SKITCH

Other Useful Skitch Tools

There are many other useful tools you can select to mark-up images. The menu to the right of the screen includes a list of these features:

- a blurring tool to make your students' faces blurry (to protect their identities)
- emoticons
- a stamp tool (for "X marks the spot")
- a free-form drawing tool
- a shape tool

The menu to the left of the screen includes these features:

- eight colors
- five line thicknesses

The menu at the top of the screen includes these features:

- undo
- crop
- rotate
- clear all annotations

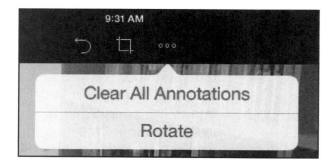

This Is Where I Sit in Class

Lesson Objective

Students will learn how to manipulate an image using annotation tools. They will then share this image using Mail.

Materials and Preparation

- one iPad per student
- one teacher iPad and projection or streaming technology

Take a picture of your classroom. Make sure your shot includes every student's desk. Send this picture to each student's Mail address. Have students save the image to their Photo Libraries.

Opening/Input

1. Launch the Skitch app.
2. Select the picture of the empty classroom.
3. Annotate the image with an arrow to indicate where you sit in the classroom.
4. Now annotate the image by adding your name at the base of the arrow using the text tool.

Guided Practice

Pick a volunteer to demonstrate the activity again in front of the rest of the class. Make sure you emphasize the "undo" icon at the top center of the app in anticipation of your students making mistakes.

On Their Own

1. Have students annotate the empty classroom image you emailed to them.

2. Once they are done, have them email the annotated image to you.

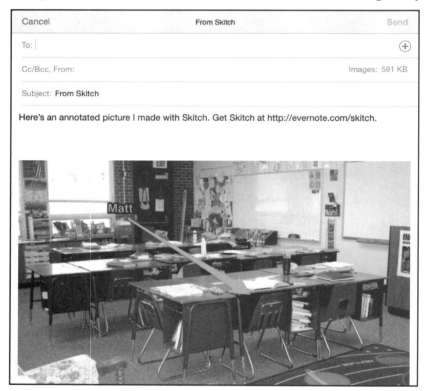

3. Share some of these emailed annotated images with the rest of the class.

Extensions

- Have your students annotate the image again, this time indicating where another student is sitting.

- Create a search game using other pictures. Take pictures of your school, and give students a list of things or places to find and label.

- Have students take pictures of themselves in order to annotate different parts of their bodies.

- Teach students how to use other Skitch tools to make their annotations more inventive.

LET'S COLOR!

Description

Let's Color! is an interactive drawing app that is designed for open-ended play. It includes extensive verbal prompts and directions to which students can respond with drawings.

How to Draw and Animate Your Drawings

1. Launch the Let's Color! app.

2. Tap on the right arrow.

3. Choose a page from the choices at the top of the screen. The scenes are all incomplete. Drawings need to be added to complete the scenes.

4. Draw with your finger. You can use the various drawing tools and colors in the bottom-left corner of the screen.

5. In the bottom-right corner of the screen is a selection of stickers to decorate your drawing. You can adjust the position and size of these stickers by tapping and dragging them and by using two fingers to rotate, increase, or decrease the size.

LET'S COLOR!

How to Draw and Animate Your Drawings *(cont.)*

6. To start the animation, tap the "GO!" icon in the upper-right corner of the screen. Watch how your drawing interacts with the scene in fun and creative ways.

7. At the bottom center of the screen is a "camera" icon. Select this to save the current drawing to your Camera Roll.

8. In the bottom-left corner is a "trash can" icon. Tap this to undo the last stroke you made with your drawing. Tap more times to undo earlier strokes.

9. The "house" icon in the upper-left corner of the screen takes you back to the app's launch screen.

LET'S COLOR!

Draw and Solve

Lesson Objective

Students will learn how to follow directions and draw pictures. Then they will share their drawings with others.

Materials

- one iPad per student
- one teacher iPad and projection or streaming technology

Opening/Input

1. Launch the Let's Color! app.

2. Explain to your students that there are three directions that need to be followed: choose a page, draw with your finger, and tap the "GO!" icon.

3. Choose a page. Say the command prompt out loud.

4. Use the drawing tools to complete the scene.

5. Demonstrate how to use the undo feature if you make a mistake.

6. Show how to add stickers to your drawing.

7. Share the image to your Camera Roll.

8. Go to your Photos app and demonstrate how to send a photo email.

LET'S COLOR!

Guided Practice

Pick a volunteer to demonstrate the activity again in front of the rest of the class. Tell the student to email the photo to you.

Note: Make sure you emphasize the undo button ("trash can") in the bottom-left corner of the screen in anticipation of your students making mistakes.

On Their Own

1. Let students use their devices to launch Let's Color!
2. Have them complete one or more of the scenes.
3. Tell them to take pictures of the finished scene(s).
4. Ask students to email you the finished scenes.

App-Smashing

Have each student use one of his or her drawings saved to his or her Camera Roll to use with Skitch. Each student can then annotate the drawing with labels denoting the parts of the drawing.

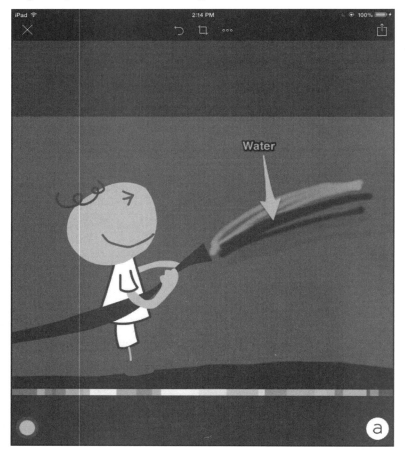

PAPER BY FIFTYTHREE

Description

Paper by FiftyThree is an innovative drawing app. It was Apple's App of the Year in 2012. The smart interface keeps the app clutter free. Included with the app is a helpful in-app tutorial, highlighting many of the app's features.

Overview

- There are three available views for the three included journals: a Journal view (main screen), a Pages view (journal is open), and a Drawing view (selected page is open). Tap and pinch to get in and out of these three views. Specifically, tap on a journal to get to a Pages view and then tap on a page to get to the Drawing view. The Drawing view is the place to start drawing.

Journal View

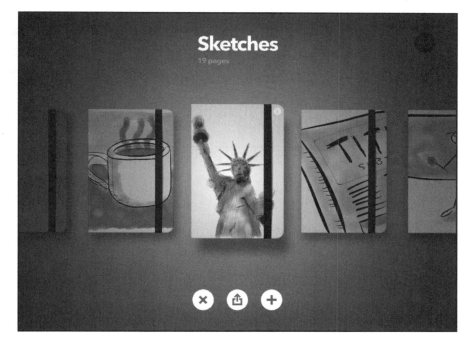

PAPER BY FIFTYTHREE

Pages View

Drawing View

PAPER BY FIFTYTHREE

Overview *(cont.)*

- To add a journal or page, select the "plus" icon on the appropriate screen.

- To delete a journal or page, select the "x" icon on the appropriate screen.

- To organize your journals with file names and book-cover images, tap on the "i" button on each journal.

How to Share and Save Drawings

- From the Journal or Pages view, tap on the "share" icon to view several sharing options. In Journal view, you can send the entire journal containing multiple drawings. In Pages view, you can send individual drawings.

- To save your drawing(s) to the Camera Roll, tap the "Camera Roll" icon. To email your drawing(s), tap on the "envelope" icon. To create a PDF, tap on the "App Store" icon.

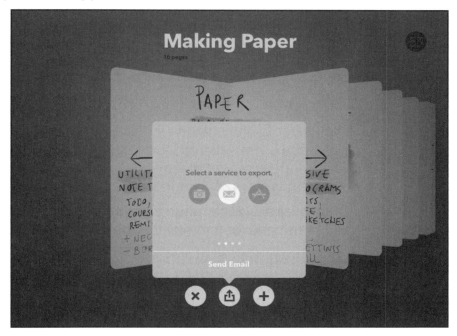

How to Draw Using Paper by FiftyThree

- Tap on the Pages view to start drawing. Use your finger to draw after you've selected a drawing tool. The faster you make your strokes, the thicker the line.

- Select different colors from the color tray in the bottom-right corner of the screen.

- Spread two fingers apart to zoom in close to your drawing without losing your place on the page. This allows you to draw fine details. Tap anywhere out of the circle to turn off the zoom feature.

- Each drawing is automatically saved in a journal.

PAPER BY FIFTYTHREE

Draw a Self-Portrait

Lesson Objective

Students will learn how to draw pictures and share them with others. Specifically, they will draw self-portraits.

Materials and Preparation

- one iPad per student
- one teacher iPad and projection or streaming technology

Opening/Input

1. Launch the Paper by FiftyThree app.
2. Show students how to "open" a journal and find a blank page.
3. Draw a self-portrait using the drawing tools. Follow the "How to Draw Using Paper by FiftyThree" instructions on page 57.
4. Demonstrate how to use the eraser.
5. Show students how to save the drawing to the Camera Roll.

Guided Practice

Pick a volunteer to demonstrate the activity again in front of the rest of the class.

On Their Own

1. Have students complete their own self-portraits.
2. Once they are done, have them save their drawings to the Camera Roll, and then have them email the drawings to you or other classmates.

Extensions and App-Smashing

- Have each student add this drawing to a Pages document and write a self-introduction. You might have your students answer the following questions: 1) What is your name? 2) What is your nickname? 3) How many people are in your family? 4) What is your favorite free-time activity?

- Have each student draw a picture of a classmate and save it to the Camera Roll. Then have the student interview that classmate using the questions above. Tell the student to create a Pages document that includes his or her classmate's portrait and answers to the interview questions.

- Have each student draw a picture of an important person in his or her life and then save the drawing to the Camera Roll. Next, have the student interview this person using his or her own interview questions. Tell each student to create a Pages document that includes the portrait and answers to the interview questions.

ART LAB BY MoMA

Description

The Art Lab app provides opportunities for open-ended exploration and creativity, as well as connections to MoMA's collection. Students can use the app with a classmate, a teacher, a parent/caregiver, or on their own. There are many interactive learning activities and prompts for creativity. Be sure pre-readers know to tap the audio button each time they need text read to them.

Note: Your Artwork May Be Used by The Museum of Modern Art (MoMA)

This app contains a feature that enables users to share their art with The Museum of Modern Art. The museum may choose to use submitted projects for their own purposes. If you share your art, please read the disclaimer below:

By sharing your artwork with The Museum of Modern Art (MoMA) or by enabling the app so that your child can share his or her art with us, you are granting MoMA a perpetual, irrevocable, fully paid worldwide right and license to display the artwork on MoMA.org, share it with the world via social media, reproduce it and distribute it in any and all media, use it for promotional, advertising, and any other purposes, and modify or change it and authorize others to do the same, for any and all purposes. If you do not agree to these terms, please do not submit your artwork to MoMA. If you do agree, please identify yourself only by first name, age, city, and country (none of which are required for submission). We regret that we cannot notify you if we intend to use your artwork. For more information, please review our Privacy Policy at MoMA.org/privacy.

©The Museum of Modern Art, New York

TAGS

Free

Classroom Contexts: Whole Class, Teacher Research, Individual, Small Group

Wi-Fi: optional (for sharing files)

Grades: all

Prerequisites: familiarity with Mail app

Developer: MoMA, The Museum of Modern Art

App Version: 1.2.2

ART LAB BY MoMA

How to Create an Art Project

1. Tap on the green "light bulb" icon in the upper-left side of the screen. You will get a prompt that suggests an activity to complete for your first art project. There are seventeen different ideas to choose from. As you swipe to the left to see the various ideas, you will notice the activities progress from simple to more advanced. Tap on the "speaker" icon at the top of the page to hear the text that is displayed. Press Go to begin an activity.

2. Tap on one of the shapes from the bottom of the screen to have it appear on the easel.

3. Pinch, zoom, and use two-finger tap to rotate the shapes.

ART LAB BY MOMA

How to Create an Art Project *(cont.)*

4. Tap on the "color-wheel" icon in the bottom-right corner of the screen to choose different colors.

5. You can also hold down your finger on a shape to access the edit panel. This will allow you to duplicate, delete, or make other adjustments to the shape.

6. Change the background color by tapping on the "double-square" icon on the right of the screen.

7. Start a new art project by tapping on the "plus" icon. Your art will be saved to the gallery.

8. If you need to clear the screen, select the "trash can" icon.

9. Tap on the "camera" icon on the right side of the screen at any time to save your drawing to the gallery.

How to Share and Email an Art Project

1. Go to iPad Settings. On the left side of the screen, scroll down until you find the Art Lab app and select it.

2. Tap on the slider to enable all sharing options (you only have to do this once).

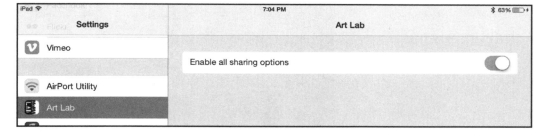

3. Return to the Art Lab app and tap on the "view gallery" icon (it looks like three squares) on the left side of the screen.

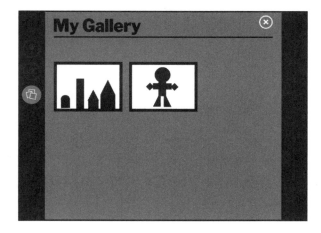

ART LAB BY MoMA

How to Share and Email an Art Project *(cont.)*

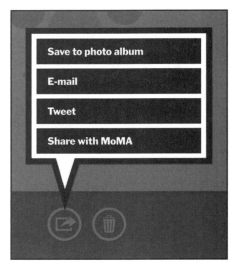

4. Select any of your previously saved art projects by tapping on the image.

5. Tap on the "share" icon.

6. Select E-mail and follow the steps to email the file.

How to Browse and Play the Art Lab Activities

1. Tap on the orange "activities" icon on the left side of the screen (it looks like a pair of scissors crossed with a pencil).

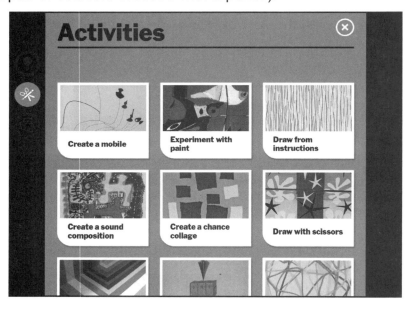

2. Browse the different activities. Notice that each activity first provides as an example a famous piece of art with a detailed description of the artist and his or her work. Tap on the "speaker" icon at the top of the screen to have the text read aloud for you.

3. Select Go to begin the guided activity.

4. You may want to preview the activities to become familiar with the various steps and to ensure they are at an appropriate level for your students.

ART LAB BY MoMA

Shape People

Lesson Objective

Students will create a piece of artwork while practicing the fundamentals of art. Students will develop an appreciation for works of art.

Materials

- one iPad per student
- one teacher iPad and projection or streaming technology

Opening/Input

1. Launch the Art Lab app.
2. Tap on the green "light bulb" icon and swipe to the second idea: "Make a person using geometric shapes (rectangles, squares, and circles)."
3. Tap on the "speaker" icon to demonstrate how the text-reading feature works.
4. Press Go to begin the activity.
5. Tap on various shapes from the bottom of the screen. Demonstrate how the shapes can be resized, rotated, and changed into various colors.
6. Arrange the shapes to create a person.

7. Be sure to demonstrate how to undo movements by tapping the undo icon (it looks like a circle around a left-pointing arrow). *Note:* You can't undo shapes, only lines. Shapes must be dragged off the screen.

Guided Practice

Invite a volunteer to come up to the front of the classroom and go through the process again. Reinforce and clarify any steps that are still not clear.

ART LAB BY MOMA

On Their Own

Allow students the opportunity to work independently. Have them launch the Art Lab app and proceed with making their geometric people.

Extensions

- You may choose to have two students share one iPad while completing this activity. Allow students to agree on an idea prompt and work together or take turns following the same prompt. Encourage them to talk about their work and their artistic decisions.

- Provide feedback to your students. Talk about what your students made. Ask questions about how they started, the choices they made, and where they got their ideas. Encourage younger students to name the shapes, lines, and colors they see.

- Now try completing some of the art activities without using an iPad. Plan ahead by gathering the physical materials needed, such as paper, tape, wire, or other art supplies.

SHADOW PUPPET EDU

Description

The Shadow Puppet Edu app lets you capture and share student work. Using existing photos and video clips from their Camera Rolls or Photo Libraries, students of any grade level can make videos to tell stories, explain concepts, or record progress. This app can also be used as a teaching tool. Create and share short lessons, explanations, and instructions, and have them available to your students anytime online or in class.

How to Access Shadow Puppet Edu's Tutorial

1. From the main screen, tap on the icon in the upper-right corner that looks like a question mark in a circle.

2. Select Show tutorial. Four helpful steps are illustrated.

How to Create a Video

1. Launch the Shadow Puppet Edu app.

2. Select Create New to start a new video. Choose videos and/or photos from your Camera Roll and Photo Library. You can also do a Web search. You can add up to 100 items to your video and record up to 30 minutes of footage.

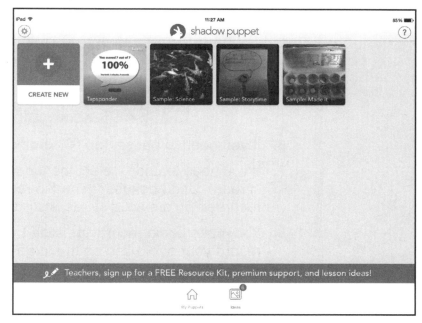

TAGS

Free (Use up to 100 items per video and record up to 30 minutes.)

Classroom Contexts: Whole Class, Teacher Research, Individual, Small Group

Wi-Fi: optional (for sharing movies)

Grades: all

Prerequisites: familiarity with Mail app

Developer: Shadow Puppet Inc.

App Version: 2.8.1

SHADOW PUPPET EDU

How to Create a Video *(cont.)*

3. Tap on the video clips and/or photos, one by one. They will appear in the order you tapped on them. These are now slides in your project.

4. If you need to reorder them, tap on Reorder and arrange the videos and photos in the same way you would organize apps on an iPad. Once you have selected and put your videos and photos in order, tap on Next in the bottom-right corner of the screen.

5. Select Start at the bottom of the screen to begin recording. You will be given a three-second prompt. Start recording your voice. A timer will appear showing you a running timer of your recording. The large right-facing arrow icon will display a gray circle that gradually becomes blue the longer you record. A good general recording practice is to record 15 seconds maximum for each slide. When the circle is completely blue, it's been 15 seconds.

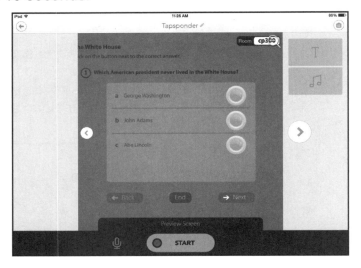

6. If you need to pause, tap Recording at the bottom of the screen.

7. If you need to undo, select the "undo" arrow in the bottom-left corner of the screen. Undo deletes the audio recording of the current slide. Anything recorded on previous slides is still saved.

8. You make audio recordings slide by slide. To go to the next slide to record your audio, tap on the large right-facing arrow icon. The next slide will appear.

9. Select Save when you are done recording. The Preview & Share window will pop up.

10. You can preview your video once again by tapping on the right-facing "play" button displayed over your project.

11. To save your video to your Camera Roll, select Done in the upper-right corner of the Preview & Share window.

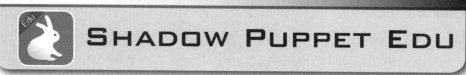

Slide Size Format

Shadow Puppet Edu formats your slides into a square format. If parts of your slides are cropped off, you can go though each slide before recording and pinch and/or zoom your image to show what you need to show.

Tap on the right-facing arrow to go forward to your next slide and tap on the left-facing arrow to go backward. All this can be done before recording begins.

How to Add Text to Videos

1. Before you start recording, you can add text to your current slide by tapping on the "T" button in the upper-right corner of the screen.

2. You can adjust the font size, style, and change the text's color.

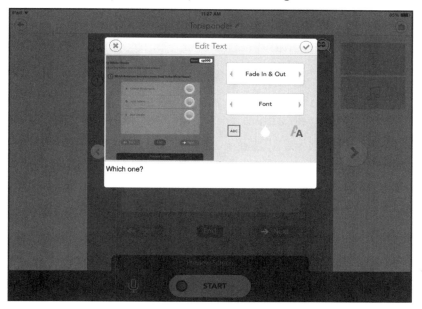

3. You can also change the way the text initially appears on the slide. After selecting your preferences, tap on the "check mark" icon in the upper-right corner of the window and choose from one of the given options.

How to Add Music to Your Videos

You can add songs from your iTunes library or choose background music provided by Shadow Puppet Edu. Simply select the "music" icon and choose either iTunes library or Background Music. Follow the steps for each.

How to Add Effects While Recording Videos

To use emoticons or the highlighter, select the "magic wand" icon. This icon will appear once you start recording the audio part of the video.

To zoom in and out, double tap on an area of the image shown.

SHADOW PUPPET EDU

Search the Web for Images

In addition to adding your own personal images from your Photo Library, you can add images from the app's own in-app education image browser. Choose images from the Library of Congress, NASA, Wikimedia Commons, Open Clipart, and others. You can also search the Web to add images to your videos. Safe-search filters are in place. You have the option to disable education-search images and Web searches entirely if you wish, since safe-search filters are never foolproof.

How to Disable Education and Web Searching

1. Go to Settings on your iPad.

2. Scroll down on the left until you find the Shadow Puppet Edu app. Select it.

3. Tap on the slider until Disable Edu or Web Image Search is green (on).

How to Share Your Videos

1. Go to the top-right corner and tap on the icon that looks like two horizontal lowercase *i*s in a circle.

2. Select Share.

3. A tray of options will appear. Choose the one that meets your needs.

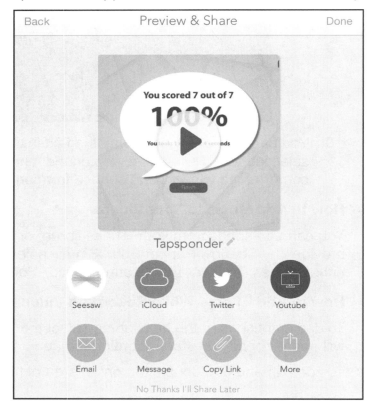

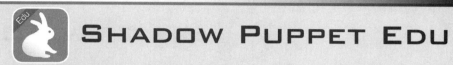

Lesson Ideas

Shadow Puppet Edu provides many lesson ideas. On the first screen, after launching the app, tap on Ideas to see a comprehensive list of lesson ideas aligned to the Common Core State Standards. Below are alternative lesson ideas that meet standards CCSS.ELA-LITERACY.W.K.6, CCSS.ELA-LITERACY.W.1.6, and CCSS.ELA-LITERACY.W.2.6, among others.

"Student Portfolio"

This is a teacher lesson. You can make a digital portfolio of all the schoolwork your students have done throughout the year. First, create a plan to identify the pieces of student work you want to include in the portfolio. Take pictures of the student work, or if they are digital, open up the files and take portrait (versus landscape) screenshots of them. Add text, noting the names of the projects and dates. If doing a whole year's worth of work is too daunting, then focus on doing an individual portfolio, such as a writing portfolio or an art portfolio.

"News Report"

Have older students find news articles and search for supporting images to help summarize them. To help students with this project, create a project template they can use during planning.

"Counting/Alphabet Practice"

Have younger students record their voices while counting numbers or reciting the alphabet. At the same time, they can use the highlighter to write the numbers or letters. For a background image, select the notebook paper in the Other section of the image browser.

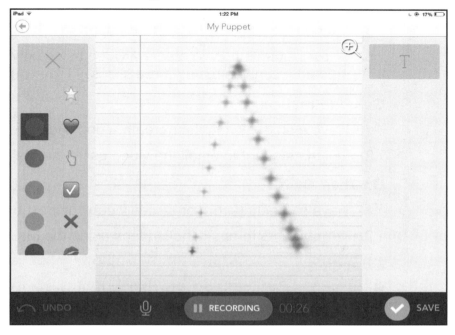

SHADOW PUPPET EDU

Digital Book Reports

Lesson Objective

Students will learn how to create digital book reports.

Materials and Preparation

- one iPad per student
- one teacher iPad and projection or streaming technology
- one storybook per student
- sample script (see below)

Create a sample digital book report as described in the Opening/Input.

Opening/Input

1. Have each student read a storybook.
2. Have students take pictures of the storybook covers.
3. Tell students that they will be giving digital book reports on their storybooks.
4. Provide a sample script (see below) that students can use for their recordings.

> My name is _____ and I read a [funny, silly, sad] book called
> _____. It was written by _____.
> I like this book because _____.

5. Launch the Shadow Puppet Edu app.
6. Show students how to create a video using only one slide. (For older students, consider using three slides.) Play your prepared sample.

Guided Practice

1. Have a student volunteer create a one-slide video about a storybook.
2. Tell the student to email the video using the Mail app.

On Their Own

1. Have students record one-slide videos using the cover photos and scripts.
2. Tell students to email their videos using the Mail app.

Extension

Have first- or second-graders do this activity using five or more slides.

Guess Who?

Lesson Objective

Students will learn how to create short videos to describe people. Then they will guess their classmates' mystery people.

Materials and Preparation

- one iPad per student
- one teacher iPad and projection or streaming technology

1. Choose a famous person as your subject.
2. Think of three facts about this person. Find three to five pictures that depict these facts.

Example

President Abraham Lincoln

Facts: He lived in a log cabin; he wore a stove-pipe hat; he loved America and was president.

Opening/Input

1. Play your "Guess Who?" video. Have your students try to guess who it is.
2. Once they have guessed it, show how you made the video, step by step.
3. Show your students how to use the image search function to find appropriate pictures.

Guided Practice

Have a student volunteer create a short video describing another person. Help your volunteer find appropriate pictures.

On Their Own

1. Have each student pick his or her mystery person, search the Web for three to five pictures, and then create his or her own video.
2. Pair up students. Have students guess each other's mystery person.

Extensions

- Require more slides.
- Have the mystery person be another classmate.
- Have students add music from the Background Music selection.
- Have students add text to their slides.

PUPPET PALS HD

Description

Puppet Pals HD is a fun, digital storytelling app that allows you to use your own pictures from your Photo Library as the actors in a story.

How to Create a Digital Puppet Show

1. Launch the Puppet Pals HD app.

2. First, you will be prompted to choose an actor (you can have up to eight). Tap on the character to add it to your puppet show. To deselect an actor, simply tap on the character's image again.

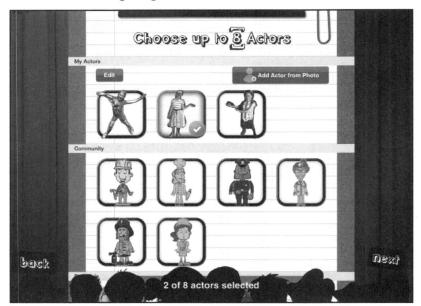

PUPPET PALS HD

How to Create a Digital Puppet Show *(cont.)*

3. A Next icon will appear in the bottom-right corner of your screen. Select Next once you have completed your character selection.

4. Now, choose a backdrop for your puppet show (you can have up to five). The backdrops you select can be changed throughout your show.

5. Tap Next again. You should now be able to see the characters you selected standing in front of one of your selected backdrops. You are almost ready to record your digital puppet show.

6. Use your finger to move the actor within the frame of the backdrop. Your final puppet show will only include the characters and the action that occur within the parameters of the background frame. Other characters are simply "offstage."

PUPPET PALS HD

How to Create a Digital Puppet Show *(cont.)*

7. After doing this a few times to practice, try using multiple fingers to simultaneously move multiple characters. Using two fingers on the same character, pinch and zoom the image to resize it, or twist your fingers to rotate the character back and forth. You can also double tap the actor to reverse its image from one direction to the other.

8. If you have multiple backdrops, you can switch between them by tapping on the tassels at the top center of the screen (You can also switch backdrops live while you are recording).

9. Think about what you want to say and what you want to do and, when you are ready, tap on the red "record" icon at the top of the screen. Your voice and the actions of the actors are now being recorded.

10. If you need to pause, tap on the yellow "pause" icon. Tap the "record" icon to continue recording.

11. Tap on the white "stop" icon to end the recording. To preview your recording, tap on the green "play" icon at the top of the screen.

12. When you are done with your digital puppet show, select the icon that looks like a little floppy disk with an arrow pointing down. You will be prompted to create a title.

13. Select the red Save button. A popup window will confirm that your recording is saved. The app will then take you to the Saved Shows screen. Here you can either play or export your previously saved shows.

14. Select the Export button to send your video to your Camera Roll. You will find your completed video in your Photos app.

PUPPET PALS HD

Going Deeper

You can choose to use the stock actors or backdrops, or you can use your own photographs to add more characters or backdrops.

When choosing an actor or a backdrop, you will be given the option to add an actor/backdrop from Photo. To add an actor, tap Add Actor from Photo and you will be given two options: Take a Photo or Choose an Existing Image. If you choose Take a Photo, the Camera app will automatically open. Use your iPad to take a photograph as you normally would. If you tap Choose Existing Image, a screen will appear displaying a collection of images from your Photo collection. Tap on an image to select it, and then use the following screen to isolate the character from the background. Use your finger to trace around the character to create and define the puppet figure. Use the Reject button if your tracing is not accurate and try again. Tap Accept when you've finished tracing your character.

To add a backdrop from Photo, follow the same steps as above.

PUPPET PALS HD

The Wacky Weather Report

Lesson Objective

Students will plan, write, and perform a weather-report puppet show using digital tools. Students will practice organizing information gathered from Internet sources, create a script, and perform a humorous news weather report on an iPad.

Materials

- one iPad per student (or group) with Puppet Pals HD app, Camera app, Mail app, Safari browser, and Photos
- one teacher iPad and projection or streaming technology
- "Wacky Weather Storyboard" template
- *Cloudy with a Chance of Meatballs* by Judi Barrett

Opening/Input

1. Explain the Wacky Weather Report project to your students. To help build excitement for the activity, you can share and read the book *Cloudy with a Chance of Meatballs*.

2. Make a list using the Pages app (or Notes) and project onto the screen all of the different possible things that can fall out of the sky. Anything is possible—including teachers!

3. Next, using the Wacky Weather Storyboard template like the one below, have your students compile a list of things that they want to report are falling out of the sky during their Wacky Weather Report.

Wacky Weather Storyboard

Name of Wacky Weather Reporter: _____

Name of town where the Wacky Weather Report is given: _____

List of animals, things, and people that are going to fall out of the sky:

_____

---

4. Once students have filled out a template like the example above, go outside and have them take pictures of the school playground. This will be the backdrop for their Wacky Weather Reports. Also, have students begin taking pictures of things in the classroom, and/or other people. With your permission, students can also search the Internet for additional images for their reports. Make sure they are only searching for images of the items they wrote down on their lists.

PUPPET PALS HD

Opening/Input *(cont.)*

5. Once your students have enough pictures (four or five), they can fill out the script below:

> *"Greetings from <u>name of town.</u>*
>
> *I'm <u>name of student</u> with <u>name of school</u> News.*
>
> *Today, there have been reports of strange weather patterns that <u>name of town</u> has never seen before.*
>
> *As you can see, <u>names of animals, things, or people</u> are starting to rain down from the sky.*
>
> *It is advised that residents of <u>name of town</u> stay inside until this wacky rain stops.*
>
> *This is <u>name of student</u>, reporting from <u>name of town</u> with <u>name of school</u> News.*
>
> *Back to you, <u>name of teacher</u>."*

Guided Practice

Ask a student volunteer to fill out the template above (or one of your own creation). Discuss different scenarios and funny materials that could fall from the sky. Encourage participation from every student.

On Their Own

1. Students must first fill out the Wacky Weather Storyboard template. Allow students sufficient time to compile a funny list of items, collect images of the items (either by using a camera or the Internet), and take photographs of the school playground.

2. Next, have students fill out a script similar to the example above. Have them practice reading their scripts silently, and then out loud to a partner to practice fluency.

3. Launch the app. Walk students through the process of creating characters, backdrops, and maneuvering the characters. Once students are ready, they can record and save their Wacky Weather Reports.

4. Allow students the opportunity to share their Wacky Weather Reports with the rest of the class.

Extensions

Students can use the Puppet Pals HD app to reinforce content in almost any subject matter. A few suggestions:

*   Have actors act out a scene from a popular Reader's Theater story.

*   Recreate a favorite scene from a recent book or story.

*   Create a humorous reenactment of a famous historical event.

PUPPET PALS HD

My Three-Part Story

Lesson Objective

Students will plan, write, and perform a three-act puppet show with digital tools. This could be an extension of a paper-based project in which you "reward" your students who have completed their paper versions with access to Puppet Pals HD to transfer their stories to a digital format.

Materials

- one iPad per student with Camera app and Mail app
- one teacher iPad and projection or streaming technology
- paper storyboard template

Opening/Input

1. Begin by discussing what makes a good story. Ask students to think about their favorite book or movie, and then share what they think makes it so good. Is it the characters? The setting? The problem? The solution to the problem? Ask questions appropriate for the grade level. Collect as much information as possible, then organize your data onto a graphic organizer. Help the students organize their comments into categories (setting, characters, problem, solution, etc).

2. Next, guide the students through the process of creating their own three-part stories. Each story should have an introduction, a specific problem, and a solution to the problem. Again, depending on the grade level of the students, the stories can be very short and simple. Help the students by guiding them through a template like the one below:

> *Part 1—Introduction*
> - What is the name of the main character?
> - What does he/she do?
> - What is the setting?
>
> *Part 2—Problem*
> - What happens to the main character?
> - How does he/she feel about what happened?
> - What does the character do to try and solve the problem?
>
> *Part 3—Resolution*
> - Is the character able to solve the problem?
> - How does he/she solve the problem?
> - Do you think the problem will happen again? Why or why not?

PUPPET PALS HD

Guided Practice

1. Using the template, walk the students through a familiar example. A book recently read by the class or a popular fairy tale would work well. Encourage the students to work with partners or in small groups to answer the questions in the template. Discuss any areas of confusion or disagreement.

2. Again working in front of the class, model an original story by following the same template. Ask the students to help provide the characters, problem, and solution. Post the new story in an area visible to all of the students.

3. Model transforming the template into a puppet show. Use the characters to act out the problem and solution of your story. If students are unfamiliar with the Puppet Pals app, walk them through the process of creating a digital puppet show.

On Their Own

1. Closely monitor the students as you release them to work on their own projects. Encourage collaborative discussions, particularly for those students who appear to be struggling with their stories.

2. As students finish filling in their templates, put them on display around the room. When most/all of the students are finished, have them share their original ideas with the rest of the class. (Many students will hear something that will inspire their next story!)

3. Allow students to use their completed templates to create brief puppet shows. Have them use their devices to work independently or in small groups. Completed puppet shows can be shared via email or projected in front of the class.

Extensions

- Once students are comfortable creating a three-part story, encourage them to attempt a four- or five-part story.

- Have students work in small groups and choreograph an entire puppet show, assigning different characters to different students.

- Have multiple students/groups use the same story to create their own Puppet Pals HD performances. Discuss the similarities and differences between the final puppet shows.

COMIC LIFE

Description

The Comic Life app helps you create simple comics, from single-page posters to multi-page classroom portfolios. The app opens with a view of all your comic creations. There is also a helpful reference manual that describes the basic functionality of the app. It covers how to create comics and how to view and share your comic creations. The tools and how to use them are very similar to the stock Pages app.

How to Create a Comic

1. Tap the "plus" icon in the upper-left corner of the screen. A tray of options will appear.

COMIC LIFE

How to Create a Comic *(cont.)*

2. Select the Create Comic option. This will take you to Comic Templates.

3. Swipe to view the different templates. Select one. From this template, you have access to other similar templates. To view these options, tap on the "dog-eared page" icon and select Template.

4. To adjust your layout, tap on the "dog-eared page" icon and select Layout.

5. Tap on the text boxes to enter text. Resize the boxes as needed.

6. Tap on the picture boxes to take pictures or add photos from your Photo Library. Resize the boxes as needed.

How to Create a Comic *(cont.)*

7. Tap on the "landscape" icon to add pictures or shapes to your template.

8. In the tabbed pane at the bottom of the screen, tap on speech bubbles to add them to your template. From there, you can also add additional text boxes and lettering.

9. Once you have finished creating your comic, tap on the "wrench" icon for Share and Print options.

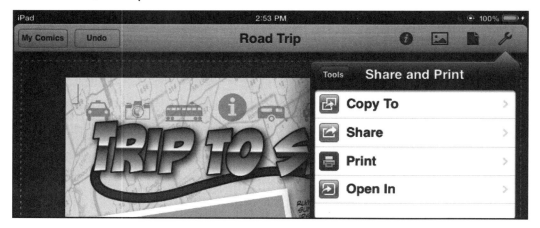

Create a Comic

Lesson Objective

Students will create posters describing themselves using digital design and layout tools.

Materials and Preparation

- one iPad per student
- one teacher iPad and projection or streaming technology

1. Create your own personal poster following the steps for "How to Create a Comic" on pages 80–82. It is helpful to have these steps displayed in the classroom, electronically or otherwise.

2. Help your students prepare the following:
   - a self-portrait photo or drawing
   - a photo or drawing of each student's favorite food
   - a photo or drawing of each student's favorite animal
   - a photo or drawing of each student's favorite activity

Suggestion: These pictures can be taken or drawn using the Camera app or the Paper by FiftyThree app.

Opening/Input

1. Launch the Comic Life app.
2. In the My Comics view, show the personal poster that you created.
3. Go through the "How to Create a Comic" steps, one by one.
4. Share your poster as an email.

Guided Practice

Ask for a student volunteer to slowly go through the steps for "How to Create a Comic." Remember to teach how to use the "undo" button to undo accidental taps and mistakes.

On Their Own

Have each student launch the Comic Life app and create a poster. Then ask students to email you their posters.

Extension and App-Smashing

- Have each student create a personal portfolio using multiple comic pages. He or she can devote one page to favorite foods, another page to favorite activities, and a third page to favorite animals.
- Have each student turn his or her comic into a puppet show using Puppet Pals HD.
- Have each student annotate his or her comic using Skitch.

Teacher Tools

As teachers, locating and organizing information for a new lesson or unit can be overwhelming at times.

This section highlights a few apps that are designed to help consolidate and organize the vast amount of information provided on the Internet. Hopefully, they'll make your life as a teacher a little easier, or at least a bit more organized!

ZITE

Zite

Description

Zite is a free news aggregation tool for your iPad that gives you complete control over the types of articles that appear in your newsfeed. You can choose from hundreds of topics, and indicate the topics that interest you most. Zite searches millions of articles daily and delivers to you only the most relevant, based on your interests. The app is very easy to navigate, and allows you to either browse through the articles quickly or save them to a separate app (such as Pocket) for later reading.

How to Set Up a Zite Account and Start Browsing

1. Launch the Zite app.

2. Select Sign-Up and provide the required personal information. Be sure to write down your login and password.

3. Now you need to tell Zite what topics you would like to read more about. You can select from the topics displayed, or you can go to the upper-right corner and do a search. Once you select a few topics, Zite will start populating your Feed (your browsing window).

4. The articles are displayed in an easy-to-read grid format. Swipe through the articles and read each title to determine if an article interests you or not.

5. Tap on an article that you'd like to read. You can read it in the app or save it to a separate app (like Pocket) to read it later—even without an Internet connection.

6. To save the article, select the "share" icon in the bottom-right corner of the screen. You will be given a list of choices. You can send an email of the URL or copy the URL to paste it elsewhere. You can also select Pocket. This will send the article to your Pocket app.

TAGS

Free

Classroom Context:
Teacher Research

Wi-Fi: required

Grade: n/a

Prerequisites:
Pocket app

Developer Info:
Zite, Inc.

App Version: 2.6

POCKET

Description

Pocket is a free website bookmarking tool that allows you to organize and read articles that you have previously saved from other apps and marked to "read later." Users can save to Pocket from over 800 different apps (such as Twitter, Flipboard, and Prismatic), or even from your Mac® or PC. Use Pocket with the Zite app to browse and then save articles, videos, and Web pages to view later—even when you're offline.

How to Set Up a Pocket Account

1. Launch the Pocket app.

2. Select Sign-Up and provide the required personal information. Be sure to write down your login and password.

3. If you have marked articles in Zite, then they will appear as readable articles in Pocket.

4. Browse your articles at your leisure. Once you are finished reading an article, you can either share it, delete it, or leave it on your iPad for future reference.

Use Pocket on Your Mac and PC

You can also format your Mac or PC's Web browser to be able to mark articles to be sent to Pocket. (The steps vary depending on your particular browser's characteristics, so go to *getpocket.com* to learn more about how to format your particular computer.) You can save any article that doesn't have a Pocket button by emailing the link to *add@getpocket.com*.

TAGS

Free

Classroom Context: Teacher Research

Wi-Fi: optional to sync articles; not needed to read articles

Grade: n/a

Prerequisites: Zite

Developer Info: Read It Later, Inc

App Version: 5.6.3

SHARING SERVICES

This section provides a few suggestions on how to share online some of the projects you'll be creating with your apps. Not only will this enable you to share activities and ideas with students, parents, and other teachers, but it will also prevent using up all of the memory on your iPad. Try several of these suggested sharing services to see which one works best for you.

Your iPad has its own memory capacity, but over time, this space can get filled up. The lessons and activities in this book are designed to keep your memory footprint low, but eventually memory space will become an issue. Additionally, if you are anticipating heavy video recording, you will want to set up one or all of these free services to help minimize the impact on your device.

iCloud

As of the release of this publication, iCloud.com is an Apple service that gives you a limited amount of free storage.

Being able to access Pages, Keynote, and Numbers on any computer (Mac or PC) is a huge plus. All you need is a free iCloud account. Creating an account is as easy as setting up an email account.

Dropbox

Use the Dropbox.com service when you have files that are too large (usually video clips) to share via email. Dropbox.com creates a virtual hyperlink from your iPad to a physical hard drive on a computer. Creating a free Dropbox account allows you to place any compatible file into a designated Dropbox file folder on your computer and then access the file from your iPad.

Once you have a sharing feature from the iPad app, you can choose to have that app share the file to your Dropbox account. If all of your students have one Dropbox account set up on their devices, then they can share huge files from the designated Dropbox folder on the computer with your Dropbox app on your iPad.

How to Set Up Dropbox

1. Launch Dropbox.
2. Follow the set of prompts to set up your account.

How to Upload Photos and Video Files with Dropbox

1. You should see ellipsis (three dots) to the right of the Dropbox heading. Tap on the three dots.

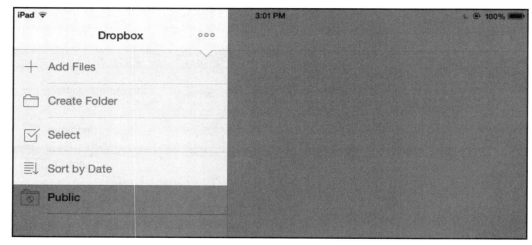

How to Upload Photos and Video Files with Dropbox *(cont.)*

2. Select Add Files. Choose the location from which you'd like to upload your photos and/or videos. They can be taken from your Camera Roll, iCloud storage, or Google Drive.

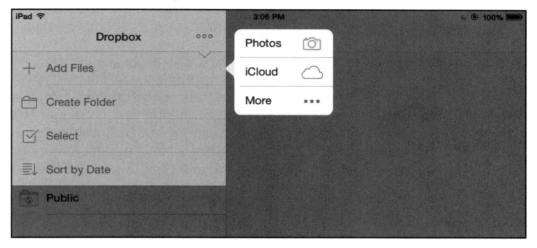

3. Tap on the photos or videos you want uploaded.

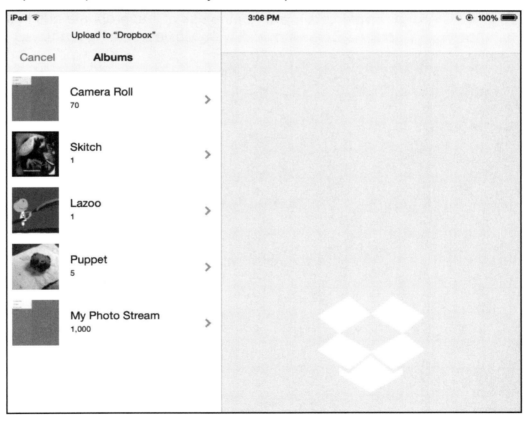

4. Once a small checkmark appears, select the Upload button (to the right of the Camera Roll heading). Your files will then upload to Dropbox.

Box.net

Box.net is similar in function to Dropbox, although you don't need a computer with designated hard-drive space to have a designated file folder. Box.net keeps your files on a virtual hard drive in the Cloud. When you share a file to Box.net, you send the file to their online cloud storage. Box.net provides a limited amount of virtual hard-drive space for free with incentives to get more space.

YouTube and Vimeo

YouTube and Vimeo are video-hosting services. Set up a free account at either website and have the option of sharing videos created by iMovie (and a selection of other apps) directly to these services. Both YouTube and Vimeo allow for customization, but probably the most important feature is the privacy settings. You can send a private URL to a parent, and only that video is available for viewing on your YouTube or Vimeo site.

The main difference between YouTube and Vimeo is that YouTube has a larger following. For your purposes as a teacher with privacy settings in play, this is not relevant. Vimeo hosts higher-quality videos and is free from advertisements. By viewing YouTube videos, on the other hand (even from a private URL), you run the risk of inappropriate ads in the margins of the screen. Both work well with iMovie's sharing features.

iPad Accessories and Care

The iPad is an investment. It's important to know how to take care of it by using a case and cleaning the device properly. In this section, care recommendations are discussed. Suggestions regarding styli, wireless keyboards, and stands are also provided.

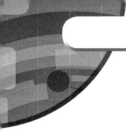

Styli

There are times when a stylus is useful, such as when you are drawing or taking notes. Unfortunately, styli are easily lost. For this reason, it is recommended that your students use their fingers when drawing and writing on their devices. Should you choose to use styli instead, make sure that they are iPad compatible.

External Bluetooth Keyboards

External Bluetooth keyboards are helpful when writing longer text. If you plan to do a lot of writing, get a full-sized external keyboard. The Apple wireless keyboard is durable and uses two AA batteries to stay powered.

Cases

Your school may have already made the decision to pack each iPad in a case. If so, review the documentation on the case so you can learn how to access all the ports and clean them.

If you have any input in the selection and purchasing of cases, then be sure to choose one that will protect the iPad if it is dropped.

Stands for Teacher Use

If you are using your iPad for whole-class presentations, then you need to prepare a place to house your iPad. Whether you are using a desk or podium, you want to make sure that you have easy access to your connection cables. These cables can become dislodged if the iPad is jiggled.

Cleaning the iPad

Newer iPad screens have become much more smudge resistant. Regardless, if students are working with them, the screens will still get smudged.

To clean your iPad screen, use a soft, lint-free cloth and wipe carefully. Do not use any abrasive cleaners or materials (including terry-cloth or paper towels).

For more information on how to clean and disinfect your iPad, go to *http://support.apple.com/en-us/HT3226*.

Each lesson and activity meets one or more of the following Common Core State Standards © Copyright 2010. National Governors Association Center for Best Practices and Council of Chief State School Officers. All rights reserved. For more information about the Common Core State Standards, go to *http://www.corestandards.org/* or *http://www.teachercreated.com/standards/*.

CCSS.ELA-Literacy.W.K.6: With guidance and support from adults, explore a variety of digital tools to produce and publish writing, including in collaboration with peers.

App	How Standard Is Met	Pages
Dictionary	searching for definitions	18–19
Pages	writing, using templates	25–30
Skitch	annotating	46–50

CCSS.ELA-Literacy.W.1.6: With guidance and support from adults, use a variety of digital tools to produce and publish writing, including in collaboration with peers.

App	How Standard Is Met	Pages
Dictionary	searching for definitions	18–19
Safari	searching for articles	20–24
Pages	writing, using templates	25–30
Skitch	annotating	46–50
Comic Life	creating comics	80–83

CCSS.ELA-Literacy.W.1.7: Participate in shared research and writing projects (e.g., explore a number of "how-to" books on a given topic and use them to write a sequence of instructions).

App	How Standard Is Met	Pages
Safari	collaborating in lesson	20–24
Pages	collaborating in lesson extension	25–30
Skitch	collaborating in lesson	46–50
Art Lab by MoMA	collaborating in lesson extension	59–64
Puppet Pals HD	collaborating in lesson	72–79

CCSS.ELA-Literacy.W.2.6: With guidance and support from adults, use a variety of digital tools to produce and publish writing, including in collaboration with peers.

App	How Standard Is Met	Pages
Dictionary	searching for definitions	18–19
Safari	searching for articles	20–24
Pages	writing, using templates	25–30
Skitch	annotating	46–50
Shadow Puppet Edu	creating short videos	65–71
Puppet Pals HD	preplanning, using the lesson template	72–79
Comic Life	creating comics	80–83

CCSS.ELA-Literacy.SL.K.5: Add drawings or other visual displays to descriptions as desired to provide additional detail.

App	How Standard Is Met	Pages
Pages	writing, using templates	25–30
Skitch	annotating art	46–50
Let's Color!	creating art	51–54
Paper by FiftyThree	creating art	55–58
Art Lab by MoMA	creating art	59–64
Shadow Puppet Edu	producing visual narratives/descriptions	65–71
Puppet Pals HD	producing visual narratives/descriptions	72–79

CCSS.ELA-Literacy.SL.1.5: Add drawings or other visual displays to descriptions when appropriate to clarify ideas, thoughts, and feelings.

App	How Standard Is Met	Pages
Pages	writing, using templates	25–30
Skitch	annotating art	46–50
Let's Color!	creating art	51–54
Paper by FiftyThree	creating art	55–58
Art Lab by MoMA	creating art	59–64
Shadow Puppet Edu	producing visual narratives/descriptions	65–71
Puppet Pals HD	producing visual narratives/descriptions	72–79
Comic Life	producing short comics	80–83

CCSS.ELA-Literacy.SL.2.5: Create audio recordings of stories or poems; add drawings or other visual displays to stories or recounts of experiences when appropriate to clarify ideas, thoughts, and feelings.

App	How Standard Is Met	Pages
Pages	writing, using templates	25–30
Skitch	annotating art	46–50
Paper by FiftyThree	creating art	55–58
Art Lab by MoMA	creating art	59–64
Shadow Puppet Edu	producing visual narratives/descriptions	65–71
Puppet Pals HD	producing visual narratives/descriptions	72–79
Comic Life	producing short comics	80–83

Apps:

Art Lab by MoMA, description 59

Art Lab by MoMA, lesson 63

Camera, description 17

Comic Life, description 80

Comic Life, lesson 83

Dictionary, description 18

Dictionary, lesson 19

iMovie, description 31

Keynote, description 42

Let's Color!, description 51

Let's Color!, lesson 53

Mail, description 11

Mail, lesson 14

Pages, description 25

Pages, lessons 28, 29

Paper by FiftyThree, description 55

Paper by FiftyThree, lesson 58

Pocket, description 86

Puppet Pals HD, description 72

Puppet Pals HD, lessons 76, 78

Safari, description 20

Safari, lesson 23

Shadow Puppet Edu, description 65

Shadow Puppet Edu, lessons 70, 71

Skitch, description 46

Skitch, lesson 49

Timer, description 16

Zite, description 85

iPad Basics:

care and cleaning 92

organizing apps 7

projecting images 9

restarting your device 9

screen capture 8

searching for apps 7

select, copy, and paste 8

switching between apps 7

troubleshooting 9

use and availability 5

iPad Accessories and Care:

cases and stands 92

external Bluetooth keyboards 92

styli 92

Permissions, student photos 6

Permissions, website 5

Tags:

Classroom format

individual 11, 16, 17, 18, 20, 25, 46, 51, 55, 59, 65, 72, 80

small group 11, 16, 17, 18, 20, 25, 46, 51, 55, 59, 65, 72, 80

teacher research 11, 16, 17, 18, 20, 25, 31, 42, 46, 59, 65, 80, 85, 86

whole class 11, 16, 17, 18, 20, 25, 31, 42, 46, 51, 55, 59, 65, 72, 80

Cost, free apps

Art Lab by MoMA 59

Camera 17

Dictionary 18

iMovie 31

Keynote 42

Let's Color! 51

Mail 11

Pages 25

Paper by Fifty Three 55

Pocket 86

Safari 20

Tags *(cont.)*:

Cost, free apps (cont.)

Shadow Puppet Edu 65

Skitch 46

Timer 16

Zite 85

Cost, free with in-app purchase options

Puppet Pals HD 72

Cost, paid apps

Comic Life 80

Developer

Apple Inc. 11, 16, 17, 18, 20, 25, 31, 42

Evernote 46

FiftyThree, Inc. 55

Lazoo Worldwide LLC 51

MoMA, The Museum of Modern Art 59

plasq LLC 80

Polished Play LLC 72

Read It Later, Inc 86

Shadow Puppet Inc. 65

Zite, Inc. 85

Wi-Fi, required

Box.net 90

Dropbox 88

iCloud 88

Safari 20

Vimeo 90

YouTube 90

Zite 85

Wi-Fi, optional (needed for sharing or other features)

Art Lab by MoMA 59

Comic Life 80

Dictionary 18

iMovie 31

Keynote 42

Mail 11

Pages 25

Paper by FiftyThree 55

Pocket 86

Puppet Pals HD 72

Shadow Puppet Edu 65

Skitch 46

Wi-Fi, not required

Camera 17

Let's Color! 51

Timer 16

Sharing Services:

Box.net 90

Dropbox 88

iCloud 88

Mail 11

Vimeo 90

YouTube 90

Wi-Fi 5